MW01233108

Monique's experie
writes with poign............
effortless authenticity. She is gifted in her ability to
weave together raw events with touching insights in a
way that genuinely invites the reader into deeper joy
and freedom.

—MATT CARDER
PASTOR, COMMONWAY CHURCH

Dancing With the Trinity is a beautiful, well-written
and entrancing book. It reaffirms how wonderful
and heart-wrenching our own dance through life can
be. This is a story that needs to be told. It pulls you
in and touches you with its honest, relatable, and at
times, emotionally raw life experiences, through the
eyes of the author. The reader will no doubt walk away
transformed."

—CINDY INGRAM

It is hard to put into words what you will find in these
stories, but I'll try. There is depth in these stories; a
deeper awareness of God, the human condition, and
human connections, I hope you feel them. There are
gifts for you in these stories; some joy, some wonder,
some loss, some sadness, I hope you find them and
open them. There are some answers in these stories;
but mostly there are questions, questions that you've
long wondered about but are afraid to ask, but you'll
find that even in the absence of answers, there is
healing. Finally there are melodies and harmonies and
movement; and I, like Monique, hope you dance.

—DR. JERRY E. DAVIS
DIRECTOR, GRADUATE COUNSELING PROGRAM
PROFESSOR OF COUNSELING, HUNTINGTON UNIVERSITY

I invite everyone who wishes to dance every day in the Spirit of the Lord to dance with these beautiful stories that Monique has so genuinely choreographed in her testimony. In hearing about Marianna, I am reminded of a dear friend who once told me of a passage in the scriptures. "Even a child maketh himself known by his doings." Listen carefully to children. Children have a way of opening our eyes up to the joys and lessons around us. Marianna is a true inspiration of love and kindness in this world and whose light cast a path that enabled Monique to dance with the Trinity in a most loving and gentle manner. It is a true heartfelt inspiration for us all to witness Monique's dance with such passion, conviction, and inner peace.

—Dr. Jerry Isikoff
Executive Director,
Liberty Health Care's Safety First Program

Dancing
with the
TRINITY

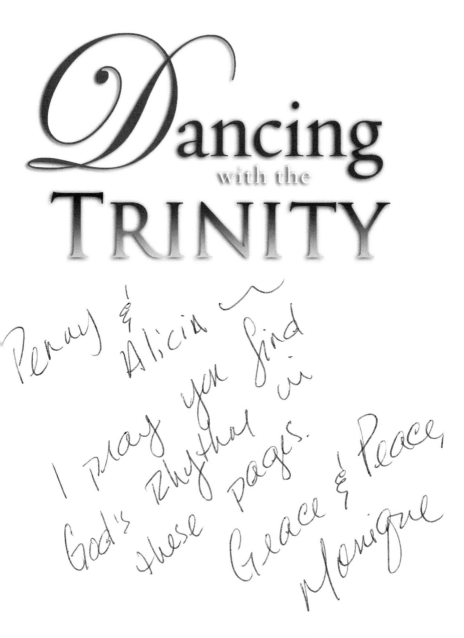

Penny &
Alicia ~
I pray you find
God's Rhythm in
these pages.
Grace & Peace,
Monique

Dancing with the TRINITY

MONIQUE JESIOLOWSKI, MA

CREATION
HOUSE

Dancing With the Trinity by Monique Jesiolowski
Published by Creation House
A Charisma Media Company
600 Rinehart Road
Lake Mary, Florida 32746
www.charismamedia.com

Unless otherwise noted, all Scripture quotations are from the Holy Bible, New International Version. Copyright © 1973, 1978, 1984, International Bible Society. Used by permission.

Scripture quotations marked KJV are from the King James Version of the Bible.

Design Director: Bill Johnson
Cover design by Ashley Willsey

Visit the author's Web site: www.lamplightercounseling.com

Library of Congress Control Number: 2011932334
International Standard Book Number: 978-1-61638-619-1

First edition

11 12 13 14 15 — 9 8 7 6 5 4 3 2 1

Printed in Canada

Dedication

For Mari: My blood, my soul, my teacher.

Because of you I understand the rhythm of my soul.

For Robert: My ezer, my beloved, my one.

Because of you I know the meaning of true love.

Acknowledgments

The Holy Trinity—They really wrote the book, I merely had the wherewithal to follow their lead.

Mari—My little five-year-old co-author. Her understanding of the Trinity and her allowance of the Holy Spirit to move and dance within her amazes me every day.

Robert—The one to always say, "Go. Write. I'll take care of…" It never would have gotten written without him.

Cindy—My "brutal honesty" girl. Her honesty is what gave me that extra little push over the edge of private writings into the realm of sharing it publicly.

Creation House (Allen Quain, Brenda Davis, Ann Stoner, Stephanie Arena, and Robert Caggiano)—all of those who poured their own sweat and blood into this book to make it the best it could possibly be. It never would have gotten published without you. Thank you.

Mom & Dad—The ones who have allowed me to stretch them even though I know it causes them pain at times.

David, wearing a linen ephod, danced before the Lord
with all his might.

—2 Samuel 6:14

Anyone who thinks that sunshine is pure happiness
has never danced in the rain.

—Author Unknown

———

Contents

Foreword

I CANNOT DANCE. THERE, I said it. It's out there. I unequivocally cannot dance. Never could, most likely never will. I've got no rhythm. Got two left feet. Got the white man's overbite. The whole bad, awkward, catastrophe thing going on. I simply cannot dance. That is why I struggled right off the bat with the main metaphor of Monique's book, *Dancing With the Trinity*. I mean, I should be right there with her, in tune with her main premise about how living one's everyday life in step with core Christian values resonates with the mind, soul, and body.

But I cannot dance. Dancing, to me, brings up images of embarrassment, fear, and potential bloodshed. So, when I read about how weaving the Holy Trinity into every word, action, and thought is like being a part of a beautiful, intricate, intimate dance…well, I had mixed emotions. I was stunned by the powerful imagery but felt embarrassment and fear well up as well. I struggled with putting my own issues aside and buying 100 percent into this book.

This book was originally titled *A Beautiful Mess*. Now, that resonated with my dance style for sure. When I try to dance, it's a mess. When I try to incorporate Jesus in my life, my efforts tend to be a mess. I can understand the metaphor of a mess…but a beautiful dance? I have never considered myself graceful enough to dance. But then, Monique's main point hits me like a cold breeze on a hot summer day; Jesus meets me there…right?

The Beatitudes are all about how He sees a dance when we see a mess. When we are poor in spirit, when we hunger and thirst for righteousness, when we choose peace, when we mourn, when we realize our humility, then He is with us. God is on our side of our mess. He takes the awkward, overbite, two-left-feet catastrophe and transforms it into a dance. *Lord, that is amazing!* When Jesus said, "It is not the healthy who need a doctor, but the sick" (Luke 5:31), I hear, "It is not the dancers who need Me, but the awkward messes."

Monique's book, *Dancing With the Trinity*, has helped me see that. The funny part is that Monique is my wife. Those experiences that she relates to explore their spiritual context? I experienced them right next to her. Yet she saw the dance. I am sorry to say that I saw the mess then, but I am glad to say that today I see the dance. I see truth in this book. Beyond whether you can physically dance in real life or consider the book a good read, I hope that you can see the truth in what she writes, because I believe that God led her to write this message to reach out to the people who feel like every move they make in life results in a mess and show them that the Lord sees a wonderful dance.

As I write, my family's day is winding down. My daughter Marianna, who is now closing in on five years old, asks a question of Monique. "Mommy, will you dance with me?" Monique swoops her up in her arms with a resounding "Yeah, baby, of course," and the dance begins anew. Maybe it is because the book has so touched me so much, but this simple action almost moves me to tears. I feel overwhelmed with emotion, because I see it for what it is, a reflection of the true essence of the love with which the Father showers us every moment. I get that now. *Dancing with the Trinity* has opened me to that.

It gets harder for Monique to dance with Marianna as she grows taller and heavier. I think how likely someday she won't be able to dance with her at all. Marianna will age to the point where she will be too big and possibly won't even want to dance anymore. Maybe she'll just be embarrassed by Mommy wanting that close dance. Or maybe the dance will survive but just change as Marianna stands on her own two feet. It is hard for me to think about that, because I so love the dance. I love the dance. I join them; I wrap my arms around both my wife and my daughter and move with them to the music. The three of us dance. It is a holy moment, but then Monique has shown me that every single moment of our lives has the powerful potential of holiness.

We move together; a thought fills my heart, body, and mind: I can dance.

—ROBERT E. JESIOLOWSKI, LCSW
CEO, LAMPLIGHTER COUNSELING
MAY 6, 2011

Author's Note

DANCE IS MOVEMENT of the body—*any* movement of the body. We usually think of dance as the type of movement that expresses a certain style of music. However, in its truest definition, every time we move, we dance. Dancing is in our nature. It is part of who we are, who God created us to be. Yet that is not how we have been taught. We have been taught to pray and worship in silence. How often on Sunday mornings do you see people busting grooves while the praise music is on? In my experience it is not too often. Usually I will see the praise bandleader kicking his heels and dancing as he sings and plays. As I look out into the audience, I see folks just standing by their seat, obediently mouthing the words that are on the screen. Is this how God wanted us to worship?

Sybil MacBeth writes about how difficult it is for her to sit in prayer in her book, *Praying in Color*:

> Most often [prayer] was done sitting down in silence with closed eyes. But my body has always rebelled against those parameters. It likes to move. Most bodies like to move. The body does not want to be rejected as the less "spiritual" part of our being.[1]

I completely agree with her. God created our bodies for a specific purpose—to worship. I feel like I am worshiping the most when my body is in sync with my heart and mind; it moves with the thoughts, prayers, and love that I pour out to God. We are made in His image and so the dance must continue. *Perichoresis* is the Greek word the early church used to refer to the Dance of God. Timothy Keller describes it this way in his book *Reason for God*:

> Each of the divine persons centers upon the others. None demands that the others revolve around him. Each voluntarily circles the other two, pouring love, delight and adoration into them. Each person of the Trinity loves, adores, defers to, and rejoices in the others. That creates a dynamic, pulsating dance of joy and love.[2]

I am a woman in her late thirties who has taken the time to process the various happenings of my life. I have come to realize that my life has been and continues to be a pulsating dance. I have ebbed and flowed with the Trinity; sometimes I danced solo, and sometimes I danced with each one individually or the collective whole, depending on what was going on in my life. That is what this book is about—my dance with the Trinity. I have come to realize that the Trinity has always been dancing with me, regardless of whether I recognized His presence.

So I will share the melody and notes of my life with you. I will share with you stories of my husband, Robert, and our daughter, Marianna. I will share how I grew up and how that has molded me compared to the way God intended for me to be molded. Robert and I own a private mental health practice, and we will share how our experience has brought extra melodies into our lives as well. I will talk about times when I made up my own dance before fully surrendering to God's. In putting down my melody—my song—on paper, I pray that healing will come not only to me but to you as well. I pray that this book helps you to find your rhythm. The more I learn about my own dance with the Trinity, the freer I become in my movements, in who I am. This dance is teaching me about who God created me to be, and I love this dance called life. I pray that this book will help free you to dance as David did—with reckless abandon.

Grace and peace,

Monique

Prologue

I AM STANDING ON my Father's feet as He guides me in my dance of life. I look down and see my black, patent-leather shoes and my lace-trimmed socks. I am in a dress, and I feel my brown pigtails swing tenderly across my face. I am always little when I am with my Father. That is how the vision goes. As I dance, I let go. I let my Father lead me where He wants me to go, and I am a willing partner. I can feel my Father's strong hands and feet as He guides me through the steps. We drift along the dance floor, and I am blown away by how smooth and rhythmic His movements are. In retrospect, I should not be surprised, for He has been dancing since the beginning of time and before.

My Father danced joyously on the day of my birth. He has guided me through my dance of life, letting me stumble yet showing me the steps over and over again until I catch on. He has wrapped His arms around me and swayed with the waves of my grief. He has waltzed with me during my times of peace and has danced the jitterbug at my highest and most spirited moments. When I have been too weary and burden laden, He has picked me up and danced my dance for me; all the while my head rested upon His shoulders, my arms wrapped around His neck.

When I am held by my Father, I can feel the rhythm of His breath, the cadence of His heart. A baby is the most peaceful lying on his mother's breast, for the mother's dance— her breath, her heartbeat—creates their connection; the baby is at peace. My Father shows me His flow of movement, and I become one with it, one with Him. Peace, love, and contentment beat within my soul. We are all part of this flow. Part of the Father. Part of the dance.

All I have to do is close my eyes and feel the rhythm of my life. For it is written on my heart, on my soul. My Father has knitted this song within my very being. All I have to do is stop and listen. The song is not only mine but also my Father's. They are woven together and cannot be separated. When my Father moves, I move. It cannot be helped.

Chapter

1

A Rainy Fall,
Faraway Places in My Living Room,
a Grand Magical Day, and
Servitude to My Daughter

———

God's "Book of Life"

I have a journal in which I write for Marianna.

I started writing it the day Robert and I decided to start a family.

I have written about the exact day and time we found out I was pregnant with her and the entire nine months of pregnancy.

I write about the major milestones in her life and the struggles we have gone through, as well as all the fun stuff that we have done together. I write about all her idiosyncrasies.

Do you ever wonder if God has a "Book of Life" like that?

Not only does it have our names written in it, but also God has written down His every thought since He created us, all the idiosyncrasies He planted in us to make us unique, the struggles we have encountered, and all of the fun stuff that we have done together.

I T WAS OCTOBER, and it had been raining for two solid weeks! I hated it! That was not fall! To me, fall is a cold breeze with the sun shining brightly, warming my face. It is the gold, red, and bronze leaves that light the sky on fire. It is wearing a sweatshirt and jeans, not a slicker and mud boots. Fall is warm enough to play outside but cool enough to elicit a nice cup of hot cider or hot chocolate when it is time to come in. Fall is my favorite season, yet I had only been outside once to enjoy it. Fall should not be a rainy, muddy mess. That would be spring.

Because it was so wet and muddy outside, Marianna and I were stuck inside, thinking up new games to play. And I was struggling. My three-year-old daughter wants to continuously play with me, and I felt pressured to play games like hide-and-seek and becoming a number of imaginary characters. That is not my forte. My forte lies outside. I love the great outdoors. I am a farm girl by nature, so I love to explore beyond my front door. I am not one to sit in a living room and imagine a forest or a faraway land. When I am inside, I want to snuggle up on the couch and read. And as an adult, when I am inside, I want to clean, bake, organize, and decorate the house. When I am indoors, I want to do grown-up things, for I am a kid at heart only when I am among the trees.

Marianna always wanted to play imaginary games with all of her figurines and stuffed animals. She could turn a living room into a space station, a dark forest, or a cattle ranch. She always wanted to include me in her games. I loved that she wanted to be with me; when I played, however, I was thinking of all the things that I needed to get done. There were dishes in the sink that needed to be put into the dishwasher. The floors could have used a vacuum. And the mud room was always a mess because that's our catch-all room. These to-do lists consumed me, and I began to feel guilty when the list grew another six lines rather than dwindled. I am a doer by nature. I would do all of my homework and then work on extra credit. If I cleaned my room, I would go through my closet and drawers to clean out things I did not need. If I ran a mini-marathon, I would train as if I were running a full-length marathon. (Admittedly, this has never actually happened since I hate running…unless it counts if someone chases me…and then only for a short duration.) I am not one to sit and do nothing. But that is how I felt when I sat and played games with Marianna: *I am sitting on my butt, getting nothing accomplished.* I felt guilty as a stay-at-home mom because Robert would come home to find the place in the same or worse disarray.

Robert would encourage me to play with Marianna. He has never once focused on my to-do lists and has never been bothered when things were not done. My guilt all came from my own head. It also came from growing up in an environment in which accomplishment was more important than play. Dad was always working, either at the electric company or on the farm. Mom always had laundry to do or a meal to prepare. My brother and I are three years apart; we would play some, but all too often Tom found himself having to help outside. Growing up in my family, getting things done was more important than playing and having fun. Now I was caught in the middle; I had a household to run and a daughter. I was caught between needing to get things done and wanting to play with my daughter.

I also wrestle with not being a "kid person." You know, those people who can be with kids 24/7, think of cool games and crafts, and make up an entire kid-friendly story with a heroine, a villain, a comedian, and an intricate plotline all off the tops of their head? I am not good with that type of stuff. I cannot do it. I volunteered this year to be a helper at vacation

Bible school for Marianna's class. It ran from 9:00 a.m. until noon, and those were the longest three hours of my day! I was mentally, emotionally, and physically exhausted by the time noon rolled around. I expressed it to one of the other volunteers, and she looked at me as though I were crazy! She responded, "Oh, honey! I could do this all day every day! This energizes me and is so easy!" *Easy? I can barely handle playing games and entertaining one child, let alone thirty of them!*

If I were asked to go to the top of a building and talk someone suicidal down, I would immediately go, talk to her as though we were best friends, and convince her to come down without so much as a question that there were options other than the one I placed in front of her. I could do that without the blink of an eye, yet I cannot come up with a craft idea that would turn construction paper into masterful pieces of art. It is just not in me.

As a result, I spent a lot of my energy trying to get Marianna to do things that I enjoyed or needed to get done. I tried to get her to help me clean the house or do laundry or to sit and read stories for hours on end. I found myself trying to talk her out of her ideas for playtime and tried to re-create them within my comfort zone. She sometimes got frustrated with me, gave up on her idea, and did it my way. *Is this the way I want my child to be raised? Do I want her to learn to give in to others' wants and desires? Do I want her to end up unsure of what she wants because others talk her into something else?* I didn't want my daughter to suffer for my issues. It wouldn't be fair. I shouldn't make her do something else so that I can maintain my comfort level. I'd be angry if anyone else did that to her.

One day I decided I wasn't going to focus on my own wants or what I needed to get done. I was going to focus on playing and spending time with my girl. I allowed her to take the lead, and we did whatever she wanted to do. Of course, we had to stop for breakfast and lunch as well as a few potty breaks, but other than that, I was all hers. By the end of the day we had trashed the joint! There were blankets strewn all over furniture in order to make our caves nice and dark. Figurines were scattered everywhere as there were casualties from the pirate fights, villains who had gotten beaten by the superheroes protecting the earth, and bad guys who were trying to steal the forbidden treasure. Stuffed animals had accumulated in the dining room, which had been turned into a zoo. Plastic cups, dishes, and silverware were spread throughout the kitchen from the royal tea party that we attended at the queen's castle.

As we began to power down for the evening, I looked around, and guilt came over me once again. Laundry was still piled up in the mud room; dishes, in the sink. Dust bunnies were all over the floor. I could have left a streak on the top of the television if I had dragged my finger across it. I felt as though I had not accomplished anything. Dinner had not even been planned, let alone started, and Robert was due home any minute. I began to regret my decision to neglect my responsibilities... until Robert came home.

When he came in through the kitchen and saw the mess, at first he looked astonished. As he continued to walk through the house and see the chaos, a smile began to appear on his face. He stopped at each station and took a moment to see what game had been played there. When he had perused all the stations, he looked at me and said, "Well, it looks like you two had a grand, magical day! I wish I could have been here to be a part of it." I felt some peace come over me, but I still felt as though I needed to explain why things had not been done around the house. Robert stopped me in mid-sentence and reminded me that my job was to take care of our little girl, and by the looks of things, I had taken extra good care of her that day.

Robert did not come home and see the house as a mess. He did not see toys strewn everywhere; he was not angry that he could not sit on the couch because Marianna's toys consumed it. Robert did not focus on the dishes in the sink or the laundry in the mud room. Robert did focus on what the mess represented. Within the mess, Robert saw a relationship strengthen between a mother and a daughter. He saw scattered toys represent my love for Marianna. He saw two people who spent the day loving each other and spending time together.

As I rocked with Marianna that night, I began to think over the day. I began to realize that I *am* a "kid person." God created me to be a mom, and He created me to be able to go off to imaginary, faraway places with my daughter. I still fought with the duties of being a stay-at-home mom. God had given us our house; I wanted to be a good steward of it. I wanted to take care of it and make sure it was clean and nice for my family. When I brought this up to God, He said, "I gave you stewardship over the most important treasure on earth, a child. It is more important to Me for you to invest in her, to love her, to cherish her, and to be with her. Spend that time with her; the other stuff will get done."

As He said these things to me, I gazed upon my sleeping daughter. Love, honor, and joy filled my heart and tears began to flow. The tears were for all the times I had not submitted to my daughter, the times I discounted what she wanted to do in order to pursue my own wants and desires. The tears were for the release of old patterns, old issues. They cleansed my soul so that I could let go of the old and make room for the new way of doing things. They were tears of gratefulness to my husband for helping me see the important things and redefine what it means to be a stay-at-home mom. And finally, the tears were for Marianna—the sadness I felt for her—because she suffered in the past when I was being selfish and stuck in my own mess. I quietly vowed to her that I would not be selfish again and that I would focus on her and on our relationship rather than on the next to-do list. That night the Holy Spirit danced with my tears as they spilled down my cheeks. He moved with the cleansing of my soul. He danced with my shame, regret, and guilt, swooping it all up into the air until it dissipated. He then reminded me of the steps to the dance of motherhood. I closed my eyes and let its rhythm fill me.

The next day as I sat on the floor with Marianna, she told me that it would be OK for me to do laundry. She said she was fine playing by herself because we played together so much the previous day. By giving her what she needed, she was filled enough to allow me to do what I needed. Marianna needed and desired me. She needed me to be with her and connect with her through play. When I did that, it filled her up. Since she felt complete, she no longer needed me so fiercely. It allowed her to let go of me a little so that I could do other things.

And I did...for about five minutes. My heart had been changed. I no longer felt the need to get things done. I felt the need to be with my daughter. So I threw in laundry and, hopefully, added the soap. I ran back to the living room and picked up my sword.

Pirates are too busy plundering treasure to do laundry!

Chapter

2

Did Jesus Want the Night Off?
Refusing to Order Pizza,
Forgetting Our Equation, and
the Sum Is Greater Than Our Parts

How God Created Marianna

One night Marianna said to Robert, "It took God a long time to make me."

Robert replied, "It did?"

Marianna said, "Yeah, He made my face, my brain, my arms, and my legs. But that's not what took so long."

Robert, intrigued, asked, "Really, what took so long to make?"

Marianna answered, "My heart. It took Him a really long time to make my heart."

Robert was surprised by this answer and asked, "What makes you say that?"

Marianna said, "Because He told me." She then rolled over and went to sleep.

A T THE TIME of writing this chapter, I am thirty-four years old with a one-year-old daughter and am just now beginning to truly understand who I am meant to be in Christ. I have struggled for many years in the shadows of my family. The emotional wounds I have carried have hindered me from truly knowing who I am and who I was meant to be. Now that I have my own family, God has really shown me what it means to be a part of the family in which I grew up and what it means to be a part of His family. God is teaching me about space and movement—within my family and within myself—so that I may be the person who God always intended for me to be. For isn't that truly what God is about: movement, creation, space?

For many years I tried to figure out whether I was more like my father or my mother. I hoped for the former and purposefully tried to be more like my father because of the misconception based on genetics and science that I would be exactly like my mother. There is this strong belief today that we are our parents, that it is inevitable that I will turn out to be like my mom and that my brother will be the spitting image of my father. We are somehow destined to become everything we hate in our parents and powerless to stop it. Yet that is a lie, for where in this theory does it talk about us being like Christ?

I am learning that God gave me my parents so that I would inherit certain traits. Sure, I have the same facial expressions as my father and exude the same mannerisms as my mother, but that has nothing to do with who God created me to be. It goes much deeper than that. He gave me parents not to become them but to meld them together to become who God created me to be. Let me explain.

I believe that my mother has intermittently struggled with a mild anxiety disorder. She has gotten nervous and scared at most new things and has restricted her world so that she can feel safe and avoid dealing with what makes her nervous. She has never admitted to our family that she has this disorder, nor am I certain that she has ever been diagnosed by a therapist or doctor. However, it is clearly evident through her actions— or, should I say, inactions. For example, she has my dad make phone calls to Pizza Hut because phone calls can be too nerve-wracking for her. She will seldom travel places on her own because it causes her too much anxiety, and she gets so nervous talking to strangers that many times she misconstrues what they are saying and answers incorrectly. Her life has revolved quite a bit around her anxiety. She has come a long way in her years, and I am very proud of her improvement in this area. I have watched her grow into someone who has traveled to Europe a few times, driven herself to the suburbs of Chicago, and reluctantly called for takeout. Often, however, her anxiety gets the best of her, shutting her out of many opportunities and experiences. God did not create her to be a scared person, but that is who my mother is at times.

To understand other people, one must start with lineage; we do not directly become who God made us to be but are influenced by those who raise us. In order for you to understand me, you must understand my family and the way I was raised. To understand my upbringing, you need to understand the people who brought up my parents. My mom has some sort of anxiety disorder. It had to have come from somewhere, and I have a pretty good guess that my grandmother had a lot to do with it.

My grandmother, Mary, was born in the 1930s on the south side of Chicago. Her mother was a prostitute. Her father was a "john." Gram, as my brother and I call her, had many half-siblings, whose fathers were all unknown strangers passing in the night, looking for a little company. When Gram was very young, she and her half-brother Bob were adopted by a family on a farm just south of Chicago who already had a biological daughter a couple of years older than Gram.

Gram grew up being ashamed of her sordid beginning, so she compensated with superficial means. She dreamed of finding the perfect husband, having the perfect family, and having the perfect house. However, making things perfect required a lot of control. My mom retells the story of how excited she was when she got new Keds shoes. They were soft, white, all the rage—and they were hers! She was by the front door one afternoon when she took them out of the box and put them on. She got five feet down the sidewalk before she realized she had forgotten something. She got half way through the kitchen before Gram slapped her across the face and told her to get those "dirty shoes off my nice, clean floor."

I too remember similar things. I can recall being about four years old, at her house, coloring with my brother on the living room floor. Within seconds Gram had ripped our coloring books and crayons out of our hands. Her guests had just arrived, and she did not want them to see a huge mess on the floor. Gram wanted to make the outside look perfect because inside her was a mess. It still is. That can certainly wreak havoc on those around you.

A few months ago we were all at my mom's house for dinner. Gram and her sister were sitting on the couch, talking about old times. There was a slight lull in the conversation, and I saw Gram staring out the picture window with a distant look on her face. Suddenly she said, "I hate how I was born." My great-aunt let out a soft gasp and replied, "Mary, you are eighty-four years old. It's time you let all of that go." Gram continued to stare silently out the picture window until dinner was called.

What saddens me about Gram's story is that she grew up in the church. She attended every week, was in the Ladies' Altar Guild, cleaned the church, and participated in many church events. She read the Bible and knew the stories, yet she knew not of Jesus's lineage. Matthew 1 describes Jesus's lineage, which mentions the names Tamar (v. 3) and Rahab (v. 5). Tamar slept with her father-in-law (Gen. 38), and Rahab was a known prostitute (Josh. 2). They were part of Jesus's heritage. Jesus also said in Matthew 21:31, "I tell you the truth, the tax collectors and the prostitutes are entering the kingdom of God ahead of you." If my grandmother could have grasped this in her teachings, then maybe she would have felt differently about where she came from and who she is. I think that was Matthew's point as well as God's. God wanted to show us that status, money, or upbringing is not what makes us worthy. It is about who we are in Christ.

The same traits of anxiety have been passed down to me through the generations. I have dealt with it differently, for I have traveled on my own, spoken at national conferences, and even called Pizza Hut once or twice (at Robert's insistence). The reason it has not taken over my life is because I have offered it up to God, relying on His strength and grace. I usually get extremely anxious prior to public speaking, but instead of allowing it take over me, I let God to handle it. (Not all the time, granted, for I am merely human, but I am learning to do it on most occasions!) My mother often does not. She holds on to her anxiety because she does not know what else to do. We may have the same traits, but that does not mean we deal with them in the same manner. I certainly could choose to allow the anxiety to control me, letting it dictate every decision in my life, but instead I ask God to set my course. You see, I may have my mother's traits, but that does not mean I am turning into her. I have a choice. I am learning that there is always a choice. I can choose to follow my mom's behavior or follow God's plan. I choose to follow God and try to become who He created me to become, hopefully someone who gives things over to Him.

In my devotions I have found that Jesus gave us an example the night He entered the garden to pray. He was scared for what was to come. He became anxious over what He was going to face. We know from Matthew 26:39 when Jesus prayed, "My Father, if it is possible, may this cup be taken from me." He also told His disciples that His "soul [was] overwhelmed with sorrow" (Matt. 28:38). He was plagued with sorrow at that time, and it was suddenly becoming too much. The situation had come to a head, and Jesus became overwhelmed with what God was asking Him to do. In His prayer Jesus asked to sit out on the next part of His dance. Yet, He knew it was part of the melody to His song. He must dance that part solo. It was the only way. He had given it to God to decide what should happen, yet Jesus had a choice. Jesus could have chosen to run. He could have taken the night off and decided to sit that one out. He also could have retracted what He had preached. He could have gone along with the Pharisees and the Romans in order to save Himself. Instead He chose to give the decision to God. He poured out all His concerns, fears, and anxieties to the Lord and then let God take care of the situation.

In my field of work, which is counseling, I see how society diagnoses, labels, and looks down upon those with traits such as anxiety. People with anxiety disorders are looked upon as being weak and unable to be the independent people we are all supposed to be. Yet God does not look at it that way. These traits are opportunities to become who God created us to be. My mother has struggled with anxiety, and at times she allows it to control her. Her life can often be dictated by her anxiety and fears. She does not always choose to give it to God. She chooses to hold on to it as though her life depends on it, because she knows no other way. Her mother did not show her how to give things to God and instead held on to her control tightly, teaching her children to do the same. Our lives depend on God, but we are very seldom taught that.

Most of the times when I feel anxious, I stop and pray, giving my fears, worries, and cares to God, allowing Him to work in my life and take care of the situation, whatever it may be. Psalm 139:23–24 says, "Search me, O God, and know my heart; test me and know my anxious thoughts. See if there is any offensive way in me, and lead me in the way everlasting." When I do this, I give Him the control and act in the way that God intended. I may have my mother's anxiety, but that does not mean that I am my mother or will become exactly like her.

It is funny to witness time and time again how God defies what society teaches. Satan would love to have us believe that we are exactly like our parents, turning into all the things that we dislike about them. This line of thinking cripples us. It does not allow for growth, movement, or creation. Instead we become stagnant, unchanging, and unyielding, all of which God did not intend us to be.

Rob Bell discusses that in his book *Sex God*:

> Each thing God creates and sets in motion is a step, a progression away from the chaos and disorder toward order and harmony. The first things God commands these people to do, then, involve the continuation of this ordering and caring for and the ongoing progression away from chaos. The universe isn't finished. God's intent in creating these people [Adam and Eve] was for them to continue the work of creating the world, moving it away from chaos and wild and waste and formlessness toward order and harmony and good. As human beings, we take part through our actions in the ongoing creation of the world.[1]

In the times that I pray when I am feeling anxious or worried, a certain peace comes over me. I become calm and enlightened that God is standing before me. This brings harmony to my world, which then transfers to others, such as my friends, families, and coworkers. They no longer become my target for releasing anxiety because my anxiety has already been given to God. However, when I allow the anxiousness to control me, it affects not only me but also those around me. I complain more, pressing others to fix the situation. I become more irritable with my friends because they are not behaving the way I want at that moment. If it has to do with work, I try to get my coworkers to do whatever is causing my anxiety. I bring the chaos into their world as well as into mine, and that moves us away from the world God intended us to continue creating.

Rob Bell talks about a progression, a movement toward something better. This is exactly what God is talking to me about as well. We are part of our parents, but not totally and fully, for we are also part of God. We often forget that part of our equation of who we are. We each have two fathers, our earthly father and our heavenly Father; when we talk about who we are, however, we usually only talk about the traits we receive from our earthly fathers and mothers and forget about the traits we receive from our heavenly Father. We also forget that God made us—not just Adam and Eve, but all of us—in His image. Therefore we have not only the traits of our earthly parents but also those of our heavenly Father as well. (How cool is that!) This is where being like Christ comes in. It transcends our earthly traits into something much more extraordinary that can overcome chaos and bring more harmony into our world.

3

Blaming Our Families, Happiness Skyrockets, Watering Camels for Love, and a Door in a Remote, Sleepy Town

———

Marianna Describes Jesus in Her Life

"Mom?" Marianna begins. "Jesus is the flower of my life."
 I answer, "What do you mean, baby?"
 Marianna says, "He's always flowering."

THE OTHER NIGHT I was reading *Fabulous Friendship Festival* by Sark.[1] I usually love her books and am often moved by her writing. However, what I read did not sit well with me. She wrote about how friendships can be so wonderful because friends are people you can choose to be a part of your family. Even though it was never outwardly stated, there was an inadvertent negative connotation regarding families. The underlying message was that someone did such a horrible job at picking families that we need to take it upon ourselves to choose people who are right for us. That thought stuck with me the rest of the night, and it made me think, "What does that say about God or God's choices for us?"

God has set up families for us to have to be with, yet that is mostly what we complain about. Comedy routines are often based on relationships and how awful they are. Sitcoms revolve around how husbands and wives live together and work around disliking each other. We do it in real life as well. Wives are referred to as "the old ball and chain," "the old lady," "the boss," "the nag," etc. (Thank goodness Robert never refers to me in any of these ways!) Husbands are referred to as "the idiot," "the old man," or "the grouch." When I asked a woman recently about her husband, she said, "You mean the one who sits on the La-Z-Boy all day and does nothing?" In one TV commercial, a woman came up to a man, asking if he was looking for a good time. The man responded by sheepishly showing his wedding ring and announcing that his good times were over. I honestly could go on and on, but you know exactly what I'm talking about.

Kids are usually seen as draining the parents' money, time, energy, and resources. Many times children are blamed when the parents do not realize their dreams. I have seen this plenty of times in counseling. I had one woman tell me that if it weren't for her son "sucking the life out of her," she would be able to do the things she was meant to do. She made it sound as if it was this boy's fault that he came into the world rather than her own. Once Marianna and I went to the hospital to visit my dad, and his roommate asked how old my daughter was. When I told him she was one year old, he responded, "That's too bad she's that young. You've got a long time before you get your life back." I was offended by the comment and saddened to know that he had two children of his own whom he couldn't wait to get out of the house so that he could "have [his] life back."

Is this really how God meant families to be? Did He truly envision families to fight, blame, and complain about each other? I am very proud that Robert and I strive very hard not to let that happen. Earlier I was reading the creation story of Adam and Eve. God created her specifically for Adam, meaning that they complemented each other; they fit. They were right for each other because what God had created was good. He created them specifically for one another, and the marriage lasted their lifetime. Lifelong marriages can be found throughout the Old Testament. The marriages that God set up were good, happy, solid marriages with two people who truly loved each other.

I've been thinking about the Old Testament and looking at modern times. How many marriages have been set up by God, and how many have been based on our own choices? When I ask couples why they decided to get married, I am amazed by some of the answers I get. One man said he married his wife because she "was a nice piece of meat." Another said, "I felt like getting married, and she was there at the time." Others have stated it was due to pregnancy, wanting to get out of their parents' houses, or being a step up from where they were. Very seldom do I get answers revolving around love, God, or knowing that the couple belonged together. We have messed up the family system through our own choices. We took something wonderful and beautiful that God has made, distorted it, and then blamed others because it did not satisfy us.

I went to college in the early nineties. I was a small-town girl with rock-and-roll roots. My family and I lived in the midst of Illinois farmland, so we should have been a generation of country music lovers. But we were located close enough to Chicago to be influenced by the rock craze. I grew up with bands such as Heart, Metallica, and Poison. "November Rose" by Guns N' Roses was our theme song at homecoming. I was a rock-and-roll girl. Still am. However, in 1994 that part of me began to change.

Just as I was a rock chick at heart, my best friend, Maria, was a lover of country. Each week she went to the local country bar, "The Purple Pride," to line dance. That was where she fell head over heels for a cowboy. In order to understand how deep she fell, you have to understand a bit about Maria. Maria grew up in an abusive household. At the age of eighteen, she signed up for the military and spent the next three and a half years in Korea. Maria was a survivor and not afraid of anything. She was the type of person to walk up to a complete stranger and learn their life story within twenty minutes. So I was a bit shocked when she came back to the dorms gushing about some guy and being unable to find the courage to express her interest in him.

After a few weeks of her incessantly talking about this guy, I got fed up. I gave her an ultimatum; if she did not call him, I would. Surprisingly, she asked me to do it. I suddenly felt as though I was back in middle school, calling a boy to ask him to the dance for my friend. Nevertheless, I took the number. Eric answered the phone, and when I had explained who I was and what I wanted, he pleasantly informed me that he had to work at the bar later that night, but we were welcome to come over beforehand.

A few hours later, we lighted upon his doorstep, ushered in by his roommate who pointed to Eric's room to let us know the guy was sleeping. Maria and I went to his doorway and politely woke him up. He apparently did not appreciate having two lovely ladies gently tear him away from his dreams because he gave some expletives in response. I let him know how rude he was before I grabbed Maria's hand and directed her back to the front door and her car.

As punishment for embarrassing her, Maria forced me to attend line dancing each week at "The Purple Pride." It is no surprise that Eric was a bouncer on every one of those nights. After a couple nights of being around each other, Eric became a little nicer, and I became less indignant. At some point we became friends. Maria had taken an interest in Eric's best friend, George, who also bounced at the bar.

A few months down the road, Maria was dating George, and I, Eric. I had been thrust into the world of country. When we were not attending classes, the four of us were always together. Since I was the only one who didn't listen to country music, I began to shift. My CD collection had begun to morph from Aerosmith and AC/DC to George Strait and Sawyer Brown. I went to various surrounding venues that hosted line-dancing events and even began to enter contests. Eric was an excellent dancer. He entered many competitions and usually won.

It began when Eric would come back from work, informing me that he had signed us up for some dance workshop or competition. I found myself just going along with it. I went so far that even my wardrobe was affected. While once I sported ripped jeans, combat boots, and concert T-shirts, my closet was now filled with Wrangler jeans, cowboy boots, and western shirts. The only thing missing was the cowgirl hat. (Thank goodness!) By May of 1995 I found myself with a bachelor's degree, a fiancé, and a new job that was five hours away from the man I loved. Being fresh out of college was a lonely time for me. Every weekend I traveled to where Eric was competing, spending all my free time doing what he loved.

By mid-October of that year, my life consisted of work and Eric's world. Because of that, I was absolutely devastated when he broke off our engagement. The biggest betrayal for me was when he said, "I just don't know who you are anymore." *How could that be!* I had become everything I thought he wanted me to be.

I remember sitting on the floor of the living room in my apartment. I was sitting there, soul-sobbing—you know, the kind that comes from the depths of your being, when every pore cries out. As the tears came, so did the anger. Not at Eric or even myself. But at God. I felt as though He was the one who took it all away because He did not love me. Among my sobs and angry cries, I heard, "This is not the life I created for you." I then began to feel a warming sensation slowly travel up my body. My tears gradually stopped as I continued to listen.

"Come. See how I have created you.

"I have made you to be more than what you have become.

"Let Me show you your own song. Come and let Me show you the dance that I have created for you."

I danced with God for the next three years. I refrained from social events, dug deep into Scripture, and prayed. When I was not working, I spent time with God. I took long drives into the country and walked around in nature, capturing the essence of God—the essence of me. He broke down the structure that I had built around myself and created a new one. It was the start of my lifelong journey to find the notes to my song. (As I write this part of my life, I must share that my daughter is wearing a cowgirl hat and boots. She is in a western phase. And so the dance continues.)

When Eric and I broke up, it was extremely painful for me. However, he was right in that God did not plan for us to be together. I realize that now. I had a friend from college ask me what would have happened if I had married him. My response was that I would be divorced, on a lot of antidepressants, or both. Marrying him would not have been what God wanted, so the answer above is true. That is why the divorce rate is so high and so many of us are on antidepressants. That is also why there are so many relationship self-help books out there, and marriage counselors have job security. Am I saying that those who married the person God chose for them are free from problems and conflict? No, of course not, for 1 Corinthians 7:28 states, "But those who marry will face many troubles in this life." We are still human and have the wonderful ability to mess things up. What I am saying is that when we are with the person whom God created for us, our chances for love, commitment, and happiness skyrocket. It's easier to work through the problems because God made it that way from the beginning. I am not saying that marriages not chosen by God are all doomed to fail, either. They can always be rectified and made good as long as God is put in charge. For we belong to a God who wastes nothing. All I am saying here is that it is through our choices that families are messed up. Families are blessed, sacred things created by God that become distorted and painful when we make choices without Him.

Looking back at my childhood, my parents did not make the best choices in raising my brother and me. I do not remember most of my childhood prior to the age of eight. Growing up in my family was a somewhat painful process, although I know that mine was not the worst by any stretch of the imagination. However, there were still parts that I never want to repeat in my own family. Yet, isn't that exactly what many of us do? We repeat the patterns from our childhood families with the spouses we have chosen, end up unhappy, and then blame our origins for our predicament. That is the exact setup of most TV talk shows. How many times on TV do we see people who are unhappy with how their lives turned out, blaming everything on their parents? We constantly see that in therapy as well. What most people do not understand is that we have the power to change the story of our lives through God.

About seven years ago I was single, and the focus of my life was finding a mate. I had traveled; I had a career, a nice apartment, and lots of friends. The only thing missing was a boyfriend. I went out on weekends, hoping to find someone even though I was miserable. I was getting close to thirty, and I was done with the party scene. Church seemed to already have everyone paired up, and my friends' brothers seemed to already be either married or engaged. My prospects were running on empty. The few guys I did date ended up being extremely self-centered or emotionally stunted. I had pretty much had it. One evening after an awful date I literally told God that I was done. I was tired, and if He had plans for me to be married, then He would have to make that happen. I told God that if He had a man picked out for me, then He would have to bring that man to my front door because I was not going out there anymore! Nice of me to dictate to God what He was going to do, I know. It wasn't my best moment. I'm pretty sure that God sighed a huge sigh of relief when I said that. Like, "Thank goodness! Finally, you're going to let Me have control. About time!" Within six months Robert showed up. When he showed up on my doorstep, I knew he was the one.

All little girls ask their grandmothers or moms how they knew that Grandpa or Daddy was the right one for them. Grandmothers and moms usually answer, "When it's the right one, honey, you just know." That does not really say a lot and does not comfort the little girl, yet it is true. I had entrusted my love life to God, and He brought Robert to my doorstep. I "just knew" because God showed me Robert was the one. When we are in tune with God and His will, then the answers become known.

In Genesis 24, Abraham wanted a wife for Isaac, so he sent

a servant back to his homeland in search of a wife for his son. Upon reaching his destination, the servant asked God that He show him the wife intended for Isaac by her response when asked for a drink of water. Rebekah had come to draw water from the well, and the servant basically asked if he could have a drink from her bucket. Rebekah complied and then also offered to give his camels water. She did exactly what the servant prayed to God that she would do; the servant knew that she was to be Isaac's wife.

The story later states that Isaac and Rebekah were married and "he loved her" (Gen. 24:67). These were two people who had never met before but married upon Rebekah's arrival. And Isaac loved her. He loved her because she was the perfect match for him. She was the one whom God made specifically for him; that is why the marriage worked. This concept is not just for ancient times; it speaks true today as well.

As I have mentioned before, Robert is also a mental health therapist. He runs men's groups at the not-for-profit agency where he works full-time. One of the men in one of Robert's counseling groups talked about how marriage comes about in his church. He said that when a man has it laid upon his heart that it is time for him to have a wife, God also lays upon his heart who that person is. The man then tells the pastor, and the pastor instructs the man to continue to pray about it. The pastor then approaches the woman, informs her what has been laid upon the man's heart, and asks her to pray about it. After some time, if it is spoken through prayer that the two of them are meant to be together, then they each approach the pastor individually, and he completes a ceremony that marks them to be engaged. The interesting part to me was that some of the men in the group thought this was restrictive.

It's amazing how God knows the hearts of all men. He knows who He created each of us to be. If it is also in our design to be with a mate, then God has created that person for each of us as well. He can bring anyone in the world to our doorstep. We are the restricted ones because we look for mates in churches, schools, bars, and other local areas. We search only as far as we can reach. Our reach is highly restricted compared to the access that God has to the entire world.

Robert and I found each other in a remote town in Midwest Illinois. If there was ever a place that had slim pickings, it was there. And yet we found each other. A few months prior to Robert showing up on that infamous doorstep, I prayed about a husband coming my way. In prayer I asked God how I would ever find a man in my dried-up, small, sleepy town. I usually prayed on my drive to work. As I was driving one day, a sensation came to my left hand. It felt as though I was wearing a ring on my ring finger. The odd thing was that there was no ring on that hand at all, let alone on that finger. It continued the entire way to work. When I pulled into the parking lot, God whispered, "It'll happen. Trust Me."

I did trust Him; Robert appeared at my door six months later.

And I couldn't be happier.

Chapter

4

A Ghost Beneath the Sheets, a Single Tear Rolls, Blowing Imaginary Kisses, and Healing on the Third Floor

---

A Trip Back to Heaven

Marianna told me that she needed to make a quick trip back to heaven.

When I asked her why, she said that she forgot to give God a big hug and kiss when she left. She explained that she was just a baby then and didn't know how to give hugs and kisses.

ROBERT, MARIANNA, AND I, along with my parents, park near the entrance of the hospital. There are a few moments of silence in the car as we prepare to go inside. We are parked on the backside of the hospital where the convent infirmary is located. My aunt, Sister Magdalene, has asked to come here to die. She has wrestled for six years with cancer. It has been a long, hard battle in which she is finally losing. We all know this, which is why it takes us a few moments to put on a brave face. We walk through the sliding glass doors, take squirts of hand sanitizer, and say hello to the receptionist. She talks with my mother and father as if they are old friends, for in many ways, they are.

We key the elevator and head up to the third floor where the dying nuns reside. As soon as the doors open, I see my other family members standing in the hallway talking. My aunt, Sister Marie, is the first to greet us, giving us hugs and kisses and expressing how happy she is that we have come. Aunt Marie is also a nun and has been residing at the infirmary with my aunt Maggie for a few weeks now. After greetings and loving salutations, the family guides me back toward Aunt Maggie's room. We live three and a half hours away, so this is the first time I have been back to see her since she returned about a month ago. They begin to warn me of how she looks and how shocking it will be for me to see her in this state. They suggest that Marianna stay outside so she won't be scared, to which we agree.

I slowly walk into the room. Aunt Maggie is a ghost beneath the sheets. She lies with her head back, short hair newly poking through, eyes closed, mouth gaping open as she battles for every breath. Her hands are neatly folded one on top of the

other. Her silver wedding band that symbolizes her commitment to Jesus glints ever so gently from the sunlight that comes
in through her window. My mom comes with me and lets Aunt
Maggie know that I am here. Aunt Maggie grunts a faint reply.
I express my love for her and ramble off updates on the happenings in my life. I mention that Marianna is also at the hospital
but down the hall, and my aunt grunts excitedly. She wants the
presence of Marianna. I let her know that I will be back with
her in a minute, and I leave hurriedly to fetch my daughter.

A couple of the family members express their concerns about
having someone so young go in to see her, for Marianna is only
three years old at this time. They fear for how it might affect
Marianna, a valid concern. After a few moments Robert and I
decide to let her go in. Robert and I can feel the Holy Spirit
fluttering earnestly around us. He is trying to cut in because
He knows that this is an important part of the dance. He
knows that the steps to this dance must be taken. And so we
know that if Aunt Maggie asked for her, then there is a need
for Marianna to be in that room. We spend a couple of minutes explaining to Marianna that Aunt Maggie is terribly sick,
so she does not look well. Marianna nods her head, indicating
that she understands and wants to go in to see her great-aunt.
Again, my mom comes with us and gently pats Aunt Maggie's
arm to let her know that we are back with Marianna. Marianna
squeaks, "Hi, Aunt Maggie," then turns to me and asks, "Aunt
Maggie's *weally* sick, Mom?" Her innocent eyes are very con-
cerned. "Yes, dear," I answer. Marianna is frozen for a couple
of seconds, then gently turns to Aunt Maggie and says, "Aunt
Maggie, I'm gonna put kisses in your heart to help make you
feel betta. Tell me when your heart is full, OK?" She then leans
down toward my aunt and begins kissing her flaccid, ashen
hand. Marianna places her own little hand on Aunt Maggie's
heart, illustrating how she is transferring those precious kisses
into the dying woman's heart. She does this over and over and

over again. A hundred kisses must have been sent into Aunt Maggie's heart that day. When Marianna is finished, she says, "Hope you feel aw' betta, Aunt Maggie." In response, Aunt Maggie becomes highly animated, her breathing increases rapidly, and she begins to grunt several times. We pause, looking down at her. Marianna asks her if she needs more kisses for her heart, and my aunt grunts.

Marianna leans down once more, blowing kisses into Aunt Maggie's heart.

I watch the scene of giving unfold, as a single tear rolls down Aunt Maggie's cheek. At that moment I know in my heart that healing has taken place through my daughter.

When Marianna and I return back to the hallway, she asks if there are other sick people that she could see and give kisses to. I approach my aunt Marie, being a willing servant of my daughter's will. Aunt Marie helps guide us to others who are in need. We stop in Sister Madeleine's room. Sister Madeleine is a nun in her nineties who can no longer walk or talk and brawls with dementia. Aunt Marie introduces us and explains to her that Marianna wants to put kisses in her heart to help make her feel better. Sister Madeleine's eyes seemed glazed over, and we aren't sure if she understands what is going on. Despite our wonder, Marianna moves forward and begins blowing kisses into her heart. After a few moments we say our good-byes and turn to leave. I am not sure whether it has made any difference, but Marianna seems oblivious to my doubt. As we move down the hallway, we hear a commotion behind us; we turn around to see Sister Madeleine trying to raise herself up. She is grunting earnestly for us to return. When we return to her bedside, Sister Madeleine makes a kissing gesture and then points at Marianna. Aunt Marie asks if Sister Madeleine needs more kisses in her heart, and the old nun nods eagerly. So Marianna very graciously and humbly provides those kisses.

More healing has been done through my daughter.

The rest of the day is spent keeping vigil by Aunt Maggie's bed, talking and spending time with family while learning about the other sisters who reside at the infirmary. After a long day, we get ready to leave. We find Sister Madeleine sitting at the nurse's station, coloring in a coloring book. Marianna and I walk by her and wave good-bye. Sister Madeleine grunts, looks Marianna directly in the eye, and points at her. Marianna, who is a little nervous and confused, stops and stares at the old sister. I witness Sister Madeleine slowly, reverently draw her hand to her mouth and then bring it outward, blowing imaginary kisses toward Marianna. Marianna pretends to playfully pluck the kisses out of the air and put them securely into her heart. Marianna then, in turn, blows Sister Madeleine kisses, and the sister plucks them out of the air around her. Each one is placed in her heart. The nurses sit, stunned. Sister Madeleine has not connected with another person in years.

On a related topic, my husband and I took Marianna to Me's Zoo a few days ago. Me's Zoo is a wonderful private zoo, a strange collection of animals from the wilds of Africa, Australia, Canada, and South America, nestled into a good old farm town in the middle of Indiana. In the middle of visiting the animals, Marianna wanted to stop at the playground and swing for a while. As we did, a family of four came to use the playground as well.

In this family was a girl about three or four years of age who wanted to slide down the slide. She ran toward the slide in her joy, leaving her parents in her dust. As she began to climb the slide, her parents yelled at her, telling her that she was going to fall and that she could not do it on her own.

Robert and I began to watch the scene unfold, and it seemed clear that the little girl was quite capable of climbing and going down the slide without incident. In her excitement, the girl continued climbing up the stairs. The mom proceeded to climb up after her and grabbed her off the slide. She then told her daughter that slides were dangerous and she would get hurt if she attempted them on her own. She went on to explain that when she was little, she had fallen off a slide and gotten seriously injured.

Now, there were two things going on here; first, this mother was ingraining her daughter with the core belief that there are things she was not capable of doing and should not even try. Second, the mother was tainting her daughter's experience due to her own experience. She was forcing her fear onto her daughter, which is a dangerous thing to do.

We should lift up, encourage, and help our children become who God created them to be. The Lord instructs us in Ephesians 6:4, "Fathers, do not exasperate your children; instead, bring them up in the training and instruction of the Lord." This passage is saying that we need to make sure that our issues do not become our children's issues. I am sure the mother in the park had a horrifying experience on a slide, but that does not mean her daughter would. I wonder how much of that little girl's essence had been squelched that day because of her mother's own fear.

By allowing Marianna's essence to shine through and not hinder her with others' or my own fear, great healing happened that day on the third floor of St. Mary's infirmary. Marianna may not understand mortality, but she understands the embracing of life. She understands connecting with another human being at all costs. She understands that life is about giving and receiving love. She understands that there is no fear of death. How many of us can say that? How often do we hinder ourselves based on fear? What if I had listened to those family members who were afraid of how seeing Aunt Maggie could have affected Marianna? Healing would have been denied. Aunt Maggie and Sister Madeleine would have been starved of the healing that was so deeply and desperately needed.

We are born without fear. We are born with the freedom to

embrace life, even if it is presented to us through the presence of death. We place fear upon ourselves or others put it upon us. Either way, fear keeps us away from so many wonderful and incredible things. Death should not be feared but embraced. Death is not the end but the beginning of something beautiful.

Sister Magdalene (my aunt Maggie) died the very next day.

My aunt Maggie had written her own eulogy. In it she talked about how cancer was a gift rather than an enemy. She writes:

> Living with cancer has been a living of the Paschal Mystery—union with Jesus in suffering, death, and resurrection. I am grateful for my cancer. I am grateful for all that led to powerful Resurrection and loving union with God.

She embraced it as a tool to learn more about God and to have a closer relationship with Him. How utterly beautiful. She was an amazing woman.

May we all set aside our fears. May we all be so open to connecting more with each other and with God. May we not hinder our children and put aside our own fears for the sake of healing for others. That day I saw the essence of Marianna. I saw the essence of Jesus within her that day as well. What a beautiful and precious gift that God has bestowed upon Robert and me. That He has bestowed upon each of us, for each of us has the capability to heal and connect in the way that Marianna did that day in the infirmary. I pray that we let go of fear in order for us to embrace.

Chapter

5

Buying Cars and Lies, Emotional Digestion, a Contradiction in Terms, and Bucking It Up

---

Marianna's Favorite Color

I asked Marianna what her favorite color was. She said, "You are, Mom. You're my favorite color."

THE OTHER DAY in my women's therapy group at my private practice, I challenged the women regarding who God created them to be. They had no idea what that even meant, as so often is the case. When describing themselves, many of them talked about depression, anxiety, fear, insomnia, business, etc. I literally could go on and on. As they were talking, I was asking in my head, "Is this really who You created these women to be, Lord?" He answered me, "This is who others have distorted them to be, not whom I created."

In looking at the stories of these women and others, it became very apparent to me that God certainly doesn't create people to be these negative things that serve no purpose except for staying stuck and unhappy. These traits become a quality of what others have put upon them. Just yesterday I was working with a guy who was severely sexually abused by his father while his mother turned a blind eye and pretended that nothing was going on. The aftereffects of his abuse have led this man to sexually immoral behavior outside of his marriage. He describes himself as no good, dirty, horrible, etc. Any negative quality of which you can think, he feels that way about himself. Yet this man is a good man. He absolutely adores and loves his wife; he is kind, thoughtful, smart, funny, etc. Just as he could go on and on with how horrible of a person he is, I could go on and on about what a kind, gentle, loving soul he is. How can there be such a contradiction?

When we are born, we are on the path to become who God created us to be. We are innocent, beautiful, special, and unique. We are then put in the care of fallible, sinful people who are not acting in the way that God intended. They pile their own personal issues, history, beliefs, and behaviors onto us. Piled onto us are traumatic experiences, pain, hurt, deceit, selfishness. It begins to bury the purity of who God created us to be. After years and years, we begin to believe the lies and cannot see who we truly are. It is buried too deep under the abuse, pain, and hurt.

A seventeen-year-old kid came into my office this weekend because he attempted suicide. He had grown up with a mom who was addicted to meth, a dad who told him that he was a mistake, and a stepdad who said that he was worthless. The only person in his life who ever gave him positive attention was his grandmother, who is now deathly ill and lives in another state. As I was sitting across from this young man, my heart was breaking because I saw none of those things with which he described himself. I saw such kindness and goodness. I saw tenderness and vulnerability, strength and character in this young man. I was seeing him how God sees him. I was seeing him how God created him. His mother's addiction to drugs was not his fault. His dad said that he was a mistake because of his own issues and failing as a father. His stepdad tore him down in order to feel better about himself, which has nothing to do with who this kid truly is. Yet this boy believes these lies. He drinks them in as truth and then feels horrible inside. He continues to digest the toxins that these people around him are feeding him and then cannot understand why he wants to die! As I heard those stories, I could hear the wailing sorrow of God's cries. I could picture God hugging Himself, rocking back and forth as He hears the pain of His children.

Story after story, person after person, it is always the same. People are hurt, miserable, and emotionally destitute—all because they digest others' lies and then do not seek the ultimate truth, which is God. They have no idea that this is not how God created them. They actually become angry at God for giving them horrible lives and creating them to be the monsters that they see themselves as. They are blind to the fact that they were created differently; they were created for something bigger, something better. The piles of lies on top of them bury their cores so deeply that they have no concept of who they are anymore. They have lost their true selves in the fortress of these lies.

Robert and I have seen this cause discord and heartbreak in marriages as well. Couples on the verge of divorce will come in for help. Time and time again we see that between the hurt and pain, there is deep love for one another. They just cannot get past the pain, hurt, and lies that reside within their hearts. Most of the hurt was caused by others prior to marriage, but arrows and daggers get thrown at spouses because no love and joy can be seen through the lies planted in their hearts so many years ago.

We have somehow lost the ability to think critically about ourselves. We have become a society that swallows whatever is given to us. We no longer take things into our hands, examine them, and make decisions about their true natures. Instead we believe when others says something is true and digest it before ever taking a good look at it. In my practice, I continuously tell my clients to take what I say and back it up against the Bible. I encourage them to challenge my truthfulness and make sure that it is parallel to God's teachings. We should do that with everything, yet how often do we really?

Actually, we do when it comes to consumerism. When we are in for a huge purchase, how long do we take to study the product itself and how that product measures up to other products? We ask around to find out whether what the seller says is true. There are research projects, books, magazines, and websites that provide massive amounts of information. For example, when purchasing a car, we compare it to other cars, look up all the statistics on it, and ask others who own that particular model how they like their cars. We find out how reliable the car is, where it comes from, who made it, how dependable the company is, and so forth. It may take us months before we actually go to the dealership to purchase the car. Why? It is because we do not want to make bad decisions. We want to make sure that we are buying what we are being told we are buying.

How often do we do that with ourselves? Some teacher in high school tells us we will never amount to anything. How often do we digest that as truth rather than examining it and making sure it is true before we purchase that statement? Why do negative comments from people who barely know us carry more weight than positive comments from people who know us well? Why aren't we going to our Creator and asking Him what is true?

Again, I think it goes back to our lack of being critical thinkers in this area. We are told to listen to our parents as well as other authority figures and do what they say. When these authority figures lament on our stupidity or worthlessness, we take it as truth. We should respect authority figures and our parents, but that does not mean that we should digest everything that they feed us. This is why God continuously says in the Bible to look to Him, to focus our eyes upward, and to seek wisdom from Him. He never says that we should look to our parents for truth. He says we are to *honor* them. Deuteronomy 5:16 says, "Honor your father and mother, as the Lord your God has commanded you, so that you may live long and that it may go well with you in the land the Lord your God is giving you." Honor is talking about one's character. Honor is a trait that describes one who shows honesty, respect, and integrity. So when God is talking about children honoring their parents, He is stating that we are to show our parents respect, to be honest with them, and to have integrity in every interaction we have with them.

Now Hebrews 13:17 states, "Obey your leaders and submit to their authority. They keep watch over you as men who must give an account. Obey them so that their work will be a joy, not a burden, for that would be of no advantage to you." To obey or be obedient means to comply or to be respectful. Submit means to yield to the control of another, to surrender. Looking at the example of a teacher saying something mean to a student, God tells us to obey and to submit. This means not to talk back to the teacher or be disrespectful. However, God does *not* tell us to swallow what we have just been told. We can politely and respect-fully leave the words lying on the ground, allowing them to be said but never taking on the responsibility of picking them up.

There are also people who speak and give us truth. Those who give us truth learn it from the Bible. I see beauty, kindness, and wonderment in the seventeen-year-old kid, the men, and all the women in my group. I can see them that way because I know the truth of the Bible. God created each one of these people, and He can only create beauty. He can only create majestic, fab-ulous things. So when I supply these people with those truths, it is because I know the truth of what God says about them.

We need to quit digesting lies that are toxic and are only going to kill us. We need to start analyzing those statements, ideas, and beliefs that people throw at us and look to find the truth in them by looking to what God has to say about it. We also need to stop caring whether these people are our parents, someone we love deeply, or someone in authority over us. They are still sinful creatures by nature, and some will hurt others to make their own pain seem less damaging.

Start looking to God for the answer. Focus your eyes upward for the truth, and rely upon that. Take the statements of others and compare them to God's statements in the Bible. I can guarantee you will find a contradiction. And I can guarantee that you will find through God's Word who you truly were cre-ated to be. You are fearfully and wonderfully made (Ps. 139:14).

Chapter

6

A Boy in the Corner, the Epidural Layer of Wants and Needs, Without Fries and a Malt, and Giggling With the Holy Spirit

---

Watching in Delight

I was watching Marianna walk up our green front steps by herself for the first time. I just sat there smiling, delighted by my daughter's continual growth.

Do you ever wonder if God feels the same way? If He sits there, watching our continual spiritual growth in delight?

SINCE MARIANNA WAS one year old, she has experienced night terrors. She would scream in terror in the middle of the night. Robert and I would run to her room to find her sitting up, eyes open, screaming and kicking. When this first began to happen, Robert and I assumed that she was awake when we found her in this state. We soon discovered that was not usually the case. She was seeing without seeing. One of us would grab hold of her and speak sweetly into her ear. She would continue screaming. Sometimes she would kick and hit us in order to pry herself away from our hold. Then we would turn on all the lights and try to shake her out of her trance. Sometimes it would take a good hour to wake her, calm her down, and get her to realize where she was and who she was with, only to have her terrors start back up again a couple of hours later.

When Marianna was two years old, she began talking of a little boy who was in the corner of the ceiling of her room. When I rocked her to sleep at night, she would look up at the corner, talking and giggling. Robert and I did not know what to make of it, so we just left it alone. The episodes eventually started to get worse. While I was rocking Marianna, she would ask me to tell the boy to go away because he was being mean. She would cover her eyes with her blanket just to get some peace from him. I would pray during these times, but my prayers were a bit meandering, for I was not quite sure for what I was praying or how to stop it.

One night Robert and I awoke to Marianna's screaming. We ran, turning the light on to see what was going on. We found Marianna in her crib, clutching her legs and screaming, "My legs! Tell the boy to stop grabbing my legs!" We prayed over her, and the ordeal stopped...until the next night. After a few months of this and having Marianna constantly sleep with us, I called my mentor, Dr. Jerry Davis, for some guidance. After several phone calls and e-mails, he determined that a demon was attacking our daughter, and we needed to spiritually clean our house, which we immediately did, with his help.

Now, I won't go into all of the details here about how we were lucky enough to have a demon enter our home or how it all came to pass. That is for another time, another book. What I will say is that my family and I literally saw the battle of good versus evil. We saw how the angels fought for our daughter and how the lyrics of prayer could move anything. It was a dance I will never forget. I will also never forget how my daughter needed my husband and me in that time of trial. She needed to see us, feel us, and be around us.

It took tangible things for Marianna to feel safe and comfortable. She needed to hear our voices and have the lights on and our arms wrapped around her. She could not go on faith that her parents were near. She needed solid, evidential proof in front of her; otherwise, her screams continued. Her nightmares shrouded her from the light. They wrapped around her and cloaked over her like a veil. It took a steady hand, a gentle voice, and a glimpse of a light to bring her back to where she belonged.

Last night as I rocked her back to sleep, I began to think about this in a broader sense. We are to rely on God. We are to have faith, hope, and perseverance that He exists and is by our side.

But sometimes that is a difficult thing, isn't it? When darkness settles on us, sometimes the silence of God or the mere absence of His physical presence hinders us, and we find ourselves like children again, reaching out for something tangible. We reach out to things that we can touch, feel against our skin, and physically hold.

Yet it never satisfies. We always find ourselves wanting more.

We are walking around in the dark, grasping at only what can be seen directly in front of us. We seek that which we can see, feel, touch, and taste, hoping for everlasting pleasure. However, even if we receive pleasure from it, it is not enough. We want more; the item we started out with must get bigger and better. Better partner, better job, bigger car, and of course, bigger house. They may satisfy the epidural layer of our wants and needs but go no further. They do not satisfy us to the core; they do not satisfy our souls or spirits.

As I sat there in the dark with Marianna, I thought about how our hearts are like plants; they need light in order to grow and transform. While we are stumbling around in the darkness searching for something to nourish us, we find ourselves dying inside instead. The only light that can sustain our hearts is Christ's light. Second Corinthians 4:6 states, "For God, who said, 'Let light shine out of darkness,' made his light shine in our hearts to give us the light of the knowledge of the glory of God in the face of Christ."

When I am right with God and seek Him in all things, my need for shopping dissipates. I do not feel the need to have that new book or CD. However, when I am not in the Word, do not choose time to pray, or feel that I am not in need of God, I can feel my heart become weary and longing. Sometimes I try to fill it with that new outfit I just bought or that next vacation we are going to take. Yet, when the clothes are worn and the vacation has just begun, I feel no more satiated. It is because I am grasping for things that are tangible but useless to the soul.

When I was pregnant with Marianna, I craved french fries and chocolate malts, which I ate at the same time. My body needed the salt of the fries and longed for the soothing taste of the malt. I was a conscientious pregnant woman, so I would rationalize how crazy it was for my body to want those things. Instead I would eat an apple or an orange. Or, maybe I would have the malt without the fries. It was no good. I still longed for and craved the fries and malt together. My longing would not stop until I went to the nearest Steak 'n Shake and ordered a chocolate malt and large fries. Only then did my body find rest and peace. I could sleep the night through because I actually gave my body what it needed.

Isn't it like that with God? God's radical ways can be perceived as not good or at least a bit bizarre. (People thought my combination of the fries and the malt was bizarre!) When Mary poured perfume over Jesus's feet, those around Him were surprised that Jesus was OK with it. Perfume was a rare commodity and too expensive to be "wasted" by using it to wash someone's feet. When Judas protested her action, Jesus answered, "Leave her alone. . . . It was intended that she should save this perfume for the day of my burial. You will always have the poor among you, but you will not always have me" (John 12:7–8). What seemed normal and rational to God seemed like a waste to others. However, this is a great testament to how our relationship with Christ should be. Many times, instead of spending time with God and seeking His will, we rationalize our meager attempts at a relationship with God by saying, "I go to church every Sunday; that's enough." Or, "I am too tired to get up early and read the Bible. It can wait until tomorrow. Besides, I read an extra verse yesterday and volunteered to coach intramural sports at church." But our souls are craving a relationship with God. Relationship is defined by these characteristics: enduring behavioral interdependence, repeated interactions, emotional attachment, and need fulfillment. When we look at this definition, can we honestly say we are in a fulfilling relationship with God? Our souls are asking for this type of relationship with God, yet instead we try to satisfy them with something else. That something else could be good for us (e.g., exercise or vacation), but that does not matter because that is not what our souls are craving.

The other night I taught a body-prayer class for just one person. I teach my students how to worship God with their bodies. I believe that God created our bodies for worship, and this is an expression of body worship that I do and teach. The student and I were going through the movements when she began having a difficult time doing them. Now this woman was very physically fit and could do body prayer better than I could sometimes! Yet that night she could not do a simple balancing stance that she had done easily in the past. I told her to sit with her legs crossed on the floor and close her eyes. We began some visualization exercises and prayer meditation. It turned out that she was having an emotional reaction to some of the movements, so we needed to work through it mentally and emotionally. She came because she felt that her body needed exercise and her mind needed some relaxation. What her body truly needed was something much deeper, and unless we went there, her worship would have been useless. Her body needed exercise, but her soul craved release.

People who have never even heard of God still crave their Creator. I see many people come through my office who have never heard of Jesus Christ but talk about how their lives are missing something. They describe this never-ending craving that they have tried to fill with sex, drugs, or consumerism, only feeling hollower and craving more strongly. This is because at their cores, their souls know what they need—their Creator. Until they give their souls what they need, they will be in that perpetual state of dissatisfaction and hunger and will feel that they are slowly dying inside.

Giving our lives to God is like having the power turned on in our souls. Light fills us, and we no longer need the material, tangible items for comfort. We feel full of the Spirit and are no longer in need of the other things because our craving has been satisfied.

As I rocked Marianna back to sleep after her nightmare, I began to pray for her. The more I prayed and rocked, the more relaxed she became. I then asked the Holy Spirit to fill her up. As soon as I prayed for this, Marianna began to giggle. The Holy Spirit had just moved through her soul. I knew immediately that Christ's shining light was in her and that she was satisfied.

When was the last time you giggled with the Holy Spirit?

Chapter

7

Knowing the Outcome
Before You Begin, the Destination Beyond,
Expert-Level Mudslides, and
Showing Me the Way

Blue Nail Polish

Marianna and Robert bumped into Robert's friend, Maria, who is paralyzed from the neck down. Maria said, "Hi," and Marianna looked at her funny.

Maria started to explain why she couldn't move and had to be in a wheelchair.

After a couple of seconds, Marianna said, "OK, but I was wondering why you're wearing blue nail polish instead of pink. Is blue your favorite color?"

Maria asked, "Don't you want to know why I'm in a wheelchair?"

Marianna just shrugged and said, "Nah. But you must like blue, huh? It's very pretty."

Today I met with a client, and our discussion revolved around what his life would be like once he became who he was meant to be in Christ. The struggle for this client was his need to know what the final destination would look like before embarking on the journey to get there. He wanted to know the end result. He wanted to know what the destination was going to look like. I had another client who was waiting for his wife to return from prison. She had been gone for a year and half and was due to be released soon. Instead of meeting this time with joy and happiness, he met it with fear and trepidation. He wanted to know what their life would be like once she had returned. They had both changed immensely in the past year and a half, and he wanted to know the outcome before the event had begun. Another client often asked me if her husband would ever give up his addictions. She remained stuck in her fear and therefore was not moving forward emotionally. She wanted a guarantee that he would be addiction-free before she totally committed to him. Even though these clients felt that they were alone in feeling this way, don't most of us want to know what we and our lives are going to look like? Don't we wish to see the outcome that God wants for us before we actually commit to living His lifestyle? Yet isn't the journey the biggest part of the Christian walk? We will never reach our destination here on Earth. That is the whole point. As Christians we are constantly evolving, diving more into the mystery, peeling away the layers, and learning about who God is, which essentially will tell us who we are.

Look at Jesus. Jesus came to Earth to walk among us. He took a journey on this earth in order to set an example, to teach, and to show us God. Then He died and ascended into heaven.

But is that where His journey ends? If we look at the Bible and at what Jesus tells us, His journey is not over. In John 16:7 Jesus says, "But I tell you the truth: It is for your good that I am going away. Unless I go away, the Counselor will not come to you; but if I go, I will send him to you." In verse 14 He goes on to say, "He will bring glory to me by taking from what is mine and making it known to you." In verse 22 He states, "So with you: Now is your time of grief, but I will see you again and you will rejoice, and no one will take away your joy." In the Gospel of Mark, Jesus talked with a high priest, who "asked him, 'Are you the Christ, the Son of the Blessed One?' 'I am,' said Jesus. 'And you will see the Son of Man sitting at the right hand of the Mighty One and coming on clouds of heaven'" (Mark 14:61–62). Over and over again Jesus makes references to Himself past the day of His resurrection. He makes various references to the days after His resurrection and to what He will be doing. Jesus has not stopped at His destination, so why should we expect to reach our destinations in this lifetime?

Now it can sound a bit daunting that we will never reach our destination in this lifetime, right? That is the hurdle my clients were trying to overcome. *Why try in the first place if we are never going to reach it?* Yet this is how God created the world in the beginning. In his book *Velvet Elvis*, Rob Bell talks about how God created the world to continue to create upon itself, evolve, and grow. God gave this world the freedom to continue to multiply and create. This implies a never-ending process; there is no mention of a stopping point.[1]

If we look at the Bible and Jesus, we should know that this process will never be realized on this earth. And that ought to be a good thing. It must not be seen as a daunting task that we will never accomplish. It must be looked at as a never-ending adventure. *Adventure* is defined as "an activity that is comprised of risky or uncertain experiences that are undertaken at least in part for the sake of physical or emotional excitement."[2]

Webster's Dictionary also states that "an adventurous activity can lead to gains in knowledge."[3] Examples of adventures would be mountain biking, skydiving, or white-water rafting. When we think of these activities, we think of them as potentially dangerous and fun things that could help our personal growth. That is why most people go on adventures; they may grow within themselves, challenging themselves to push farther than they have ever gone before. I believe that is what God intends for us when we choose to walk His path: a life full of adventure, fun, risk, and growth.

Robert and I are from the Midwest. We are talking pretty flat land, miles of cornfield with possibly a babbling brook here and there. There are no racing rivers shooting down a mountain. So when we were in Colorado a few years ago, we decided to do some white-water rafting. When we called early that morning, we signed up for the amateur route that would take place in the afternoon. We figured we would be able to experience an adventure without much danger in it. However, we did not check the weather, and when we walked out the door and found that it was pouring, we did not think anything of it. It continued to pour as we drove through the mountains. It was pouring so hard that we had to pull over a couple of times. Being from the Midwest, we had no idea how the rain, the power of the mountains, and gravity could change things.

By the time we reached the white-water rafting place, it had been pouring heavily all day, and water was gushing down the mountain, spilling into the river in which we had planned to raft. The place was called "Clear Water Rafting," yet when we pulled in, got out of the car, and walked over to the edge of the river, it was not clear at all but chocolate covered. It looked like the river that flows through Willy Wonka's factory.

The place was hopping. Some people were shopping in the store area, others were getting ready to head out onto the water, others were talking to guides about tours, and others were just coming back. As we stopped to gather our bearings, look around, and assimilate, we noticed a huge dry-erase board with several sections and different names on it. The sections were split into three categories: amateur, advanced, and expert. We scanned the board only to find that our names were not in the amateur slot but in the advanced slot. We thought there was just a mix-up and were nervous about what that meant, so Robert talked to someone to get clarification.

As I waited, I listened to those around me who had just come from the water. They were describing the current and the rapids as volatile and crazy, which, of course, raised my anxiety quite a bit. When Robert walked back over to me, I noticed that the guide was not moving our name to the amateur slot. Thus, I really began to worry. Robert explained to me that the guide thought that we were young and physical enough to handle the advanced level, and as long as we listened to the guide, we would be fine. I remember standing in the middle of the hustle and bustle at that time and beginning to pray!

We were excited for this adventure and knew we did not want to back out, but we were still afraid of what lay ahead. We had no idea what we were getting ourselves into. Our guide took us to the back room and proceeded to train us on safety precautions. It was raining so hard that it was difficult to hear most of what he said. However, I do remember hearing things like, "If you get thrown out of the boat, we won't pick you up. Just wait for the boat behind you, and they will scoop you up on their way past." Someone in the crowd asked what we were to do while waiting for the other boat. The answer? "Just hang on to something strong so the current doesn't take you." (Was that supposed to make us feel better?) Someone else made the comment, "Well, at least these life jackets will keep us safe." One of the guides responded with, "Actually, the only thing those life jackets are good for is so that we can spot your body in the water. That's why they're so bright." (I even have a

souvenir shirt with that statement written on it!) (Excuse me!
And we paid *how much* to plunge to our deaths?)

After the training we headed out to the boats. Four tourists
and one guide to each boat. The rain was still pouring down
over us; the river was still muddy and raging at quite a good
speed. While waiting for everyone to get ready to set off into
the water, we overheard two guides talking. One had just come
from a trip and was telling the other that there was no difference between the advanced and expert anymore. The rain had
come so hard and so fast that the river was above capacity and
going so fast that all of it was going to be expert level.

It was too late for us to back out at that point, so Robert
and I stood in the rain next to our boat, saying one last prayer.
During the trip our guide continuously yelled out orders telling
us how and in which direction to paddle and what to look out
for. The four of us in the boat listened diligently and did just
as he said. We danced over rapids, splashed against rocks, and
plummeted down the falls. At one time we were catapulted
into the air, almost losing a member along with our guide and
slamming down into a rock, forcing us to go backward. It was
one of the scariest and most exhilarating dances with nature
that I can remember having. The trek was crazy, fast, exciting,
and dangerous. It was the most fun I had had in a long time.

When the trip was over, we felt so exhilarated. We bought
commemorative shirts and pictures of our accomplishment. We
could not stop talking about it. We went out of our comfort
zone and grew stronger because of it. We also grew together
as a couple because it took a lot of cooperation and encourage-
ment on both our parts to work the course. It not only allowed
us to grow personally, but I think our marriage grew because
of it as well.

In thinking back on this trip, I am reminded of our
Christlike walk. It can be exciting and wonderful but also scary
and unpredictable. It is too dangerous to go it alone, so we need

guidance. We need Jesus. Jesus is our guide, directing us and steering us in the right direction. In Mark 1:17, Jesus even says, "Come, follow me…and I will make you fishers of men." He is the one who knows the course and the steps we need to take to navigate that course correctly. If we listen to what He says and do as He directs, then our course will stay straight and strong. However, if we do not listen and do our own thing, it can put us in grave danger, which is sin.

We need an expert who knows the lay of the land. Take a look at some of the true-story documentaries that are out there. Most of them have to do with a group of people who decided to venture out on their own—no guide, no familiarity with the land, no idea what they were getting themselves into. Now, in order for the story to be made into a movie, some sort of tragedy has to befall the group, doesn't it? That is the only way we would become interested. That inevitably happens when there is no guide to lead the way, no one to forewarn the group. Tragic things happen when people are ignorant of what lies before them and have no idea what certain things mean or how they work.

Wasn't it the same way for Adam and Eve? Weren't they in unknown territory with no idea about the true meaning of things? Yet they had a guide, God. He told them what they needed to know. He told them what to do in the garden, what to eat, and things like that. He also alerted them to the dangers of the new territory they found themselves in. He instructed them not to take part of the tree of the knowledge of good and evil, yet they chose to ignore His guidance and ate of the fruit anyway.

If we look at the word *guide*, we find that the word was originally taken by Old French from Frankish *witan*, meaning "show the way."[4] The phrase "show the way" means to present something, to let somebody see; it is an invitation, a suggestion, an offering. It is not coercive, intimidating, or forceful. God shows us the way He has planned for us; it is up to us whether we accept that way. Adam and Eve chose a different way, as do many people.

On the white-water rafting trip, I could have chosen a different path from the one our guide instructed me to follow. I could have paddled a different way, sat differently, or not paddled at all. Even though he was "showing me the way" to make it a safe and fun trip, I could have turned my back. I could have done things my own way. Yet, because I chose to listen and follow the guide's directions, my trip was a breathtaking, life-changing adventure. How wonderful that our walk with Christ can be the same way. Only if we take His direction can we move and create something invigorating, alive, and energizing. I'm up for that kind of adventure!

Are you?

8

Thunder Blessing,
Yucky Kisses,
One Child Praying for Another, and
That Is Healing

Marianna's Prayer

One evening Marianna, Robert, and I were at an outdoor mall, waiting for a movie to start. In the center of the mall was a huge fountain in which people throw in pennies for wishes.

Marianna asked to put a penny in the fountain to make a wish. I handed her the penny. She threw it as high and far as she could, saying, "I wish every kid in the world would get hugged and kissed."

That was my daughter's prayer.

ROBERT AND I own a private mental health counseling practice. Never in our lives did we ever dream of owning our own business. We were happy going to a job and collecting a paycheck, letting others worry about payroll, overhead, and profit.

That is, until God stepped in.

A year before I was going to receive my master's degree, God started talking to me about starting a family. Now, Robert and I had already had it planned out. We were going to wait until after I got my degree and we were more financially secure (whatever *that* meant!). I did not like God messing up our plans, so I decided to get a second opinion. I asked Robert to pray about a family and see what God told him. Thinking back, how much denial did I have to be in to think that God was going to give Robert a different answer? At the time I asked Robert to pray, I already knew the answer but was not quite ready to hear it yet, as is often the case.

Well, at that time Robert was working at someone else's private practice about an hour away from where we lived. The office was located in a professional complex. There were several grayish, nondescript buildings surrounding a beautiful pond and a gazebo area. Between clients, Robert would sit out in the gazebo and pray.

During one of his times of prayer at work, I was at home in the backyard working on our pool. It was a gorgeous, early summer evening without a cloud in the sky. I received a call from him. He proceeded to explain to me that through his prayer time he had a vision. His vision consisted of him coming down the front stairs in our home into the front hallway. In the hallway was a little blonde-headed girl about three years old, sitting on the floor coloring in a coloring book. He then saw himself tell her that she needed to color in another room, because he was getting ready to see a client.

I was amazed by this revelation. Not necessarily that we were going to start a family, because He had already revealed that to me, but the fact that Robert's vision was so crystal clear. Robert is not prone to these types of visions; he has not had one before or since. We were not only told to start a family but were given details, such as the sex of the baby and the color of her hair! I was amazed and yet totally focused on this endeavor. Robert and I discussed it a little bit more and then mutually agreed to start focusing on having a baby. As soon as we agreed, right away we heard thunder roll across the clear sky on both ends of the phone—a blessing, given in stereo. We knew at that moment that God was pleased with us.

It also did not stop there. Not only were we to start a family, but we were also to start our own counseling practice as well! Leave it to God to throw in a loopty loo! That's the last time I will ever ask for a second opinion! You apparently get more than you bargained for when you do that! Anyway, a new baby and a new company! Are ya kiddin' me? How little did I know that the two would coincide so perfectly.

We have had the practice for a few years now and have a little three-year-old, blonde-headed girl.

Robert has been seeing a six-year-old little boy, whom we will call Gary, for quite some time now. He lives with his paternal grandparents because his parents have been heavily involved in drugs and have been in and out of prison. They were currently in prison at the time Robert started seeing this little boy.

And this boy is so broken…damaged…heartbroken…a mess. Because of all of that, he is tough to take at times. He has so much emotional baggage that his behavior at times is unbearable. Yet, when you don't want to strangle him, he is one of those kids whom you just want to wrap your arms around and squeeze all your love into. If only he would sit still for five minutes!

Because of this, Robert and I see him together. His grandparents have talked about his difficulties in playing with others and learning how to share. We have brought Marianna into several sessions after much prayer and deliberation. Now, understand that there is nothing in our counseling training that would suggest that was a good idea or even something that we should consider. We felt that God wanted Marianna to reach out to him in some way, but our own parental concerns made us hesitate. What transpired has been amazing.

The first time Marianna met him, he was running around her toy area, looking at this, throwing that, yelling, and even growling at times. We were a little worried about how Marianna would react. Without hesitation Marianna walked right up to him, put her arm around his shoulder, and asked, "Whadda matter, Gawy? You hurt?" The boy stiffened under her touch as several emotions flashed across his face: shock, fear, sadness, and longing. He moved away, not acknowledging her. Of course, that did not stop our Marianna. She continued to tell him that she loved him and kept asking if she could give him a hug.

After he left, Robert and I wondered if it would be a good idea to bring Marianna to the next session. The boy seemed freaked out by her, and we were not sure whether he would want to come back. So, the next time the boy came to see Robert, we made sure that Marianna was not around anywhere. When Gary arrived, he tore through the house, looking for her. Robert tried to tell him that she was not there, but Gary would hear none of it. He just kept saying that he *needed* to see her.

So the next time he came, we had Marianna there.

She immediately said, "Hi."

He ignored her and went straight for the play therapy station.

She put her hand on his shoulder.

He cringed and moved away.

She said, "I wuv you, Gawy."

He remained indifferent.

At his next session, again he asked for Marianna. There seemed to be an urgency to it, a longing. When she appeared, his shoulders dropped slightly as relief crept into the corners of his eyes. Yet he spent the time telling her to go away, ignoring her, and being mean to her toys. Before he was getting ready to leave, Marianna ran up to him, hugged his leg, and kissed his hand. He pushed her away, saying, "Yuck!" as he wiped the kiss off of his hand.

However, his eyes were twinkling.

Between sessions Robert and I went back and forth as to whether we should continue to allow Marianna to be present during his sessions. This boy was damaged and had a lot of darkness in his soul. Was that something that we really wanted to expose Marianna to? We know that this boy was a product of his environment, but still…we needed to protect our daughter and keep her innocent for as long as possible.

But God told us, "No." This boy needed Marianna's love more than anything. Her love for him was pure and authentic, and he knew it. He did not need Robert and me to practice our therapeutic techniques on him. He needed to be loved and seen as he was. Marianna did not see his behavior as annoying. She did not see how he was going to be taxing on her or how he would affect her day. She saw a boy who was sad, lonely, and hurt. She saw a boy who desperately needed love, and she was going to do everything in her power to give it to him.

And he needed it.

Longed for it.

He couldn't do without it, which is why he always ran in, looking for her. But he also did not know how to accept it.

Marianna did not care; whenever he showed up, she continued to give him love no matter how negatively he responded to it.

One day Gary was scheduled to come and see us; however, our hearts just weren't into it. This dance was exhausting, and we were tired of its sequence. We could give a million excuses as to why, but the truth was that we would have preferred to hang out in the backyard and relax on that particular day. We tried to rectify our hearts before his appointment, but they were unchanged by the time the appointment came around. When he got here, he was in a particularly foul mood and angrier than usual. During the session Marianna was in his face more than usual as well. She continuously wanted to talk to him and put her arms around his shoulders, which he, of course, refused. She kept asking him what the matter was and repeated to him how much she loved him. Robert and I felt we had not done our best with him, but he still seemed to leave with a little more peace than he had when he arrived.

At Marianna's bedtime that evening, she fought sleep. Her soul was unsettled, and she knew sleep would not come. I sat in the rocker while Robert tried holding her as she cried and screamed. I prayed, asking God what it was that disturbed our child. He brought forth Gary's name. I asked Marianna if she wanted to pray for Gary, and she immediately said, "Yes." So the three of us held hands in a circle and offered up prayers to God for Gary and his broken heart. Upon completion of the prayer, Marianna immediately fell into a deep sleep.

She taught us so much that day.

Her heart had been right with God from the beginning. She eagerly put aside her wants and desires to bring comfort and peace to another. Her heart was open to God's prompting that He needed more from us, and she would not rest until it was given. Our daughter is not yet three years old, yet she is more in line with God's will than those who have been walking with Him for more than twenty years, including me. Maybe that is the innocence that Jesus talks about. We are not to be childlike but remain innocent. Maybe only the truly innocent can have such open hearts to God. Maybe innocence is the doorway leading to an open path toward God. I am far from innocent; I have indulged my flesh in things that have brought me farther away from innocence. It has led to a deeper struggle to follow God with my entire being. My selfishness creeps in when I know intellectually that it is not the right path.

I chose to give my best to Gary when he was here, yet it was not my best because part of me longed for self-indulgence. Marianna certainly has been selfish at times, but she is too young to understand all the implications of it yet. She is still able to separate herself from the flesh because of her innocence. So when God called upon her to do something, she was readily available.

If our prayers brought Gary any peace that night, it was because of a three-year-old, innocent little girl who was wide open to God and followed His will with her entire being. If Gary finds peace, love, and true acceptance here, then it is due to a little girl who only sees Gary the way God created him to be—loved. May we learn to be three-year-old innocents again. May we learn to follow God with our entire being when He calls us to do something for the betterment of His kingdom. May we have innocence, eyes wide open, hearts in full communication with God, and bodies to readily follow. May we see in others only what God created them to be. May we know the peace of resting ourselves in the Lord's will and falling into deep rest once we have followed through on it.

We continue to see Gary, and we continue to have Marianna occasionally attend part of the sessions. We have by no means healed the wounds that sear this boy. He is still angry and reluctant to accept compliments and will act out at the slightest provocation. However, I do believe that we have brought him something that he wants and needs, for he always wants to come; he is always eager to find Marianna and is always reluctant to leave at the end of the session. He smiles more, and Marianna is now able to provide him one hug and one kiss at the end of each session. No longer does he wipe it away or say, "Yuck!" To Robert and me, *that* is healing.

The last time I saw Gary, he said he needed to see Marianna. When I asked why, he said, "Because she loves me!"

Chapter

9

Miserable Puddles of Mud,
the Grinch,
Patching Up the Parts I Dug Holes in, and
Rocking Under the Christmas Lights

Breathing Us In

Do you ever wonder whether the reason God wants us to be still
may be so that He can hold us, just to breathe us in?

I AM SITTING IN my den on a dreary December morning. My husband is at work, Marianna is on a playdate, and I am alone in this big house. No snow—only drizzle—which does not make for holiday cheer. The house is freezing, and the ground is not filled with glistening snow but puddles of mud from all the unseasonably warm weather we have been having in central Indiana. My mood is that of the Grinch and not likely to improve anytime soon. I am on the verge of getting a cold, our holiday shopping is not yet complete, and the night was not filled with sugarplums, rather with wakeful moments of worry.

This holiday season is not totally filled with cheer and good tidings. Instead it is met with family feuds, job opportunities fallen through, and disagreements with colleagues and friends. I feel like I am geographically located in the valley part of my life journey, in which every step is met with some sort of obstacle. The road I am on is definitely under construction. It is usually my nature to sit and worry about my surroundings rather than enjoying the ride and knowing it will all come together at some point down the road. As I sit and ponder, my mind comes back to Jeff.

I met Jeff in winter, when winters were still winters with drifts a mile high and the sun glistening on the snow turning it into diamonds. I first laid eyes on him in my grandmother's living room when I was seventeen years old. He was easily six feet tall, with short, dark, curly hair and olive skin. He also had the most infectious smile I had ever seen. It went from the corners of his mouth to the crinkles of his eyes. As it turned out, he was my cousin. His father and my grandmother were half-brother and half-sister. Jeff's father moved to California soon after he left home and had never bothered to come back. Jeff's mother died when Jeff was just a toddler, and he was raised by his older sister, Beth. His dad was often gone on various jobs. (It was rumored that he worked for the Mafia in New York, which was why he was nonexistent most of the time.) When Jeff was in his twenties, he decided to look up family and found us.

Jeff and I hit it off immediately. During his week's stay, we talked for hours, explored the land, and learned everything we could about each other. When he returned home, we often mailed letters back and forth. (That was before texting and e-mailing; I know I'm old.) When I graduated high school, Jeff invited me out to Los Angeles to stay with him and his fiancée, Anne, for the summer. I readily agreed. Jeff lived in a tiny apartment off Wilshire Boulevard. He did not have a car but rode his motorcycle all around town. Jeff would get home in the wee hours of the morning from his job working as a waiter, and he would find me asleep on the couch. After work, Jeff was always in the mood to go do something. Since Anne had to get up early to go to work in the morning, I was Jeff's late-night playmate. When he got home from work, Jeff would grab the crunchiest cereal he could find, sit on the floor next to my head, and watch television while eating. When I woke up, he would giggle and say, "Oh, I'm sorry! Did I wake you?"

We would then hit the streets on his motorcycle, exploring the land in the depths of the night. We went by the Playboy mansion one night and met some interesting characters there; another night we grabbed a bunch of hamburgers from McDonald's and handed them out to the homeless near one of the viaducts. Countless nights were spent sitting on the beach, dreaming and talking. On his days off we would ride bicycles to UCLA and poke around the classrooms to see which ones we wanted to sit in on. We mostly found ourselves in a film class, watching old movies such as *The Graduate* and *East of Eden*.

A few years later Jeff and his wife, Anne, moved to New York. Anne was still in California, tying up loose ends, so Jeff asked me to come out to visit. He lived in an apartment by the old YMCA that overlooked Central Park. I went out there for four days and slept only three hours the entire time. Jeff wanted to show me everything, and that's a lot of stuff when you're in New York! The first day I was there, he took me to the subway station. He showed me a map and told me that we wanted to get to Chinatown. When I got on the subway, I turned around to find Jeff on the other side of the doors. He grinned and waved as the car pulled away. He left me to figure out how to navigate the subway system on my own. A few stops and switching of cars later, I landed in Chinatown. As I stepped out, Jeff was standing there, waiting for me with a huge grin on his face. Jeff was like that; he was always trying to push me out of my comfort zone.

During those four days we walked everywhere, talked about everything, and met as many people as we could. I remember going to a midnight movie in a theater that had originally housed burlesque shows in its early days. An elderly woman came in with a grocery bag filled with food and sat down in front of us. When the movie was over, we noticed that the woman was upset because someone had stolen her groceries in the darkened theatre. Without hesitation Jeff took the woman by the arm and led her to a café across the street. He bought her not only a hot meal but also several loaves of bread, soup, and pastries for the woman to take home. When she was sent on her way, Jeff sat next to me and just resumed the conversation we were having before we noticed the woman. I was amazed by what had just happened and wanted to talk about it. Jeff had done things like that for so many years and so often that it had become a normal part of his daily living, no need for discussion. This was his melody, part of his dance. This kind of act was so deep within his bones that it seemed to him that this was a common dance for everyone to take part in. He seemed beautifully surprised and shocked when I informed him that not everyone dances to his drum.

As you can tell by the description above, Jeff lived life to the fullest. He always trusted that things would turn out all right. He never worried about what the next day would bring; he just enjoyed what was right in front of him. Jeff died of a brain tumor in his early thirties. Until his last breath, he continued to have that huge grin on his face. He lived his life as though he had lived into his nineties. Even when he was sick, he would only talk about how blessed and joyous he felt. I absolutely loved and adored that man.

Thinking about Jeff brings me to the blessings that resonate in my life now. I go back to last night when I put Marianna down for bed. I love putting her down for bed at night and am thankful for that time with her. The house was lit only with Christmas lights; soft holiday music was playing in the background, and all else was quiet. The puppy and kitties had been put to bed, and Robert was taking a relaxing shower. I held Marianna close to me as I gave her the bottle, and in turn she held my hands tightly. Her eyes were closed, and she was sighing softly after each drink. She slowly drifted off to sleep while eating and needed to be lightly nudged to be reminded of what she was doing. Soon the bottle was empty; her slack arms drifted to her sides as she fell into sleep. I gently picked her up to put her over my shoulder, but she was so far in the depths of slumber that she did not even notice. As I think of her in my arms that night, I cannot help but have a huge smile on my face. Nothing matters but this moment right here, right now. Things can wait until another day, and I do not want to waste one more moment worrying about what cannot be changed. What I can do is enjoy *this* moment, bask in the glow of the many miracles before me, and thank God for the treasures He has bestowed upon me. He has always taken care of me and has given me no reason to doubt Him now. He is our Father and has already promised to take care of us.

In Matthew 6:25–30, Jesus gives us this assurance:

> Therefore I tell you, do not worry about your life, what you will eat or drink; or about your body, what you will wear. Is not life more important than food, and the body more important than clothes? Look at the birds of the air; they do not sow or reap or store away in barns, and yet your heavenly Father feeds them. Are you not much more valuable than they? Who of you by worrying can add a single hour to his life?
>
> And why do you worry about clothes? See how the lilies of the field grow. They do not labor or spin. Yet I tell you that not even Solomon in all his splendor was dressed like one of these. If that is how God clothes the grass of the field, which is here today and tomorrow is thrown into the fire, will he not much more clothe you, O you of little faith?

In looking back through the pages of my life, I have found that there was not one time in which God did not come through for me and my family. He has even gone above and beyond by surpassing our basic needs and providing us with so much more. I remember when Robert lost his job, and we did not know how we were going to make it. Through God he got an even better opportunity. I remember another time when God told us to start a family when we could not afford to; God gave Robert the chance to do some consulting work that paid for her entire medical bill!

Looking back on our life together thus far, I can name dozens of situations like those. Looking at how Jeff lived his life and how my infant daughter can lie slack in my arms because of her complete trust allows me to see trust in its rawest form. How absolutely incredible is that!

Thinking about these things this morning, I am now no longer the Grinch and will be in a much better mood when my family comes back to me. I know, however, that I am still in that valley and will be for a little while longer. I also know that God is right there along with me, directing traffic, showing me alternative paths, and patching up the parts in which I dug holes. And I love Him for that.

Chapter

10

Temper Tantrums,
the Forecast Fell on Deaf Ears,
the Sound of My Heart Shattering,
and a Resting Place

———

Marianna's Thankfulness

Marianna prayed to Jesus one night, "Jesus, thank You for my attitude!"

I interrupted and asked, "Why are you thanking Him for your attitude?"

"Because He gave me a lot of it!" (That, my friends, is true.) Marianna then said, "Jesus, thank You for my time-outs."

Again I interrupted, asking, "Why are you thanking Him for that?"

Marianna said, "Because He is good." (Again, my friends, that is also true.)

MY CHILD HAS lived on this earth for over a year, and I can count on one hand the number of times she has slept in her crib the whole night through. My husband and I are very stubborn, willful people, so it is only natural that Marianna inherited some of it. I just never counted on her inheriting *all* of it—from both sides!

Being a diligent parent, I read up on how to discipline children into sleeping in their cribs. One night I decided to try one of the techniques, which was comprised of me sitting next to the crib, not touching her or making eye contact with her, until she fell asleep. At first my baby tried to get my attention by babbling and laughing. She tried to reach through the crib and tickle me. Once she found out that those things were not going to work, she threw an ever-loving fit! She screamed, yelled, threw her Baby Roar Roar (her little pink stuffed lion) across the room, and kicked the side of the bed.

It took every ounce of will power in me not to pick her up and hold on to her. Instead I went to God and asked Him if I was doing the right thing. A memory of not so long ago played back in my mind...

It was Parents' Weekend at my college campus back in 1996. The dorm was aflutter with girls cleaning their rooms, hiding things they did not want Mom and Dad to know about, chatting excitedly, and primping constantly in the bathroom. My friend, Natalie, was especially excited. She was originally from Pennsylvania, and her parents were flying in especially for this weekend. Natalie could not wait for me to meet them, and we had agreed that the two of us along with our parents would spend the weekend together.

My parents had arrived that Friday night. I went to school

about four and a half hours away from my hometown, so I did
not see them frequently, but they did come to visit when they
could. Natalie's family was coming in for the first time since
she had started attending the school a year ago. They ended up
arriving right before lunch on Saturday. Natalie brought them to
my room for introductions. Her parents were extremely cordial.
It was evident that they were a wealthy family from his Rolex
and her five-carat wedding ring, matching diamond necklace,
and earring set. They were a lovely couple who humbly insisted
on treating everyone to lunch at my and Natalie's favorite restaurant, the Jackson Street Pub.

Natalie excused herself to grab her purse and freshen up a
bit before we left. She left me to tend to her parents, which
I was perfectly fine with doing. We engaged in small talk;
they inquired about my major, and I asked what they did for a
living. When a lull in the conversation came, Natalie's father
took the opportunity to ask me an odd question, "So how much
is Natalie paying you to spend the day with us?" My parents
and I were shocked. *How could this man have said that about
his own daughter?* I looked at Natalie's mom for clarification,
for some sort of answer as to why he had posed this strange
question. What I saw in her eyes was the exact same question.
I was dumbstruck. I began to laugh, thinking it was some sort
of joke. Only when my laughter was met with uncomfortable
silence did I come to understand that they were serious in what
they were asking. Luckily, my mom stepped in, explaining how
well Natalie and I had hit it off and how good of friends we
had become since the beginning of the semester. There was a
slight pause as Natalie's parents exchanged looks. Her dad then
rolled his eyes and said, cocking his head toward the door, "I
hope you know what you're doing. The first chance *that girl* has
to betray you, she'll take it." I glanced at Natalie's mom, whose
eyes were downcast but who was slowly nodding her head. A

few moments later, Natalie came bouncing back into the room, ready to go.

Needless to say, lunch was a bit awkward. My parents and I did not know how to respond to this odd family. Natalie talked endlessly about her life on campus, the classes she was taking, and her extracurricular activities. Her father would interject a question every now and then, while her mother just sat, silently flinching every time Natalie directed attention toward her. Natalie seemed to be oblivious to their behavior. After lunch, we took a tour of the campus and then headed back to the dorms. Natalie's parents announced that they needed to start heading back due to a 7:00 p.m. flight back to Pennsylvania. I must have looked astonished. I could not believe it. They had just gotten there. They had spent more time traveling than they had spent with their daughter. Natalie's face fell for about a second before she flashed a smile and said that she certainly understood.

In our hugs good-bye, her father whispered to me one final warning, "Be careful. My little one cannot be trusted. She will betray you." The forecast fell on deaf ears, for I had chosen my side. My heart was full of empathy and sorrow for my friend. The callousness of her parents had only strengthened my friendship with Natalie. I felt that it was Natalie's parents who were the betrayers, not their daughter. However, being a parent now, one thing I know for sure is that parents know their children.

It was a mid-October evening, and Natalie and I had been studying all day. We decided to take a break and go out dancing. Natalie invited her friend, Gwen, and the three of us headed out to the dance bar called "The Reg" (short for "The Regulator"). After having a couple of drinks and mingling with our friends, we hit the dance floor. While I was dancing, I noticed that a guy had come up and started dancing beside me. When I looked up at those ice-blue eyes, I was immediately hooked. I turned my body to face his, and we boogied the night away. He was one of those rare breeds of guys who felt free on the dance floor. He did not have the prefabricated dance moves that most men use to try to impress the ladies. This was a man who was comfortable in his own skin and enjoyed life. How could a girl not be attracted to that?

His name was Brian. He had gorgeous blue eyes, sandy brown hair, and a tall, thin frame. He was majoring in criminal justice in hopes of becoming a police officer. I was minoring in criminal justice, so we had a bit in common with each other. We talked and danced until closing time. Natalie and Gwen had left hours ago, realizing that I had been smitten, and therefore they were nonexistent at the moment. They just laughed at me, gave me a hug, and left. When the bar closed, we hit the local diner and talked until the sun began to peak over the horizon. We both came from small Midwestern towns, and both sets of parents were high-school sweethearts who married and continued to live in the town where they grew up. We seemed to be connected on all levels. From that day forward, we were in each other's pockets. Brian would pick me up at my dorm and walk me to my classes; he picked me up for dinner, and evenings were spent studying or just hanging out.

Brian was also great with my friends. He always welcomed them and gave me my "girl time" when I needed it. We had only been dating about a month when a family member of mine died on the same weekend that I was maid of honor in my best friend's wedding. Brian did not hesitate to come home with me, meet my family for the first time, attend a funeral, and end the weekend with a wedding. This guy was a keeper. I could feel it in my bones.

After about nine months of dating, we began to talk about marriage. We each had a couple more years of school left, so we were certainly going to wait until we graduated. But we were in the talking stage. We just knew we wanted to be together, and we could manage to wait as long as it took. The summer between my sophomore and junior years was spent making plans for our future. I worked as a waitress in a small town café; he worked at a small town police department, learning the ropes. We would travel to each other's parents' houses whenever we got time off; between those times we spent countless hours on the phone. Upon returning to school that following August, I could not wait to tell Natalie about the relationship between Brian and me. She had been there from the beginning, and I could not wait for her to know how things had progressed. She was delighted! She started buying bride's magazines for me, and we made a list of all the things needed for a dream wedding. Life was good. I had a man whom I adored and a best friend whom I could share things with.

Then the phone call came. Just as I was coming home from class, my dorm phone rang. I rushed to answer it, thinking it was Brian on the other end. It wasn't. Instead it was a woman's voice that I did not recognize. She proceeded to tell me how she had been dating Brian behind my back for over two months. I was incensed. I called her a liar, hung up the phone, and immediately called Brian, who, of course, denied it. I decided to believe him and did not ask about it again.

A couple of weeks later, I received a call from Gwen. She sheepishly launched into a story of how she shares a criminal justice class with Brian and saw him walk out of class holding a girl's hand. I had known Gwen for a couple of years now and had not known her to lie, so this information floored me. I automatically thought back to the phone call I had gotten from that girl awhile ago. Again I confronted Brian, and again he denied it. Even though I desperately wanted to believe him, a shadow of doubt had begun to creep into my heart.

The doubt crept in further when I get another call from a girl, also claiming to be dating Brian. She informed me that they shared a couple of criminal justice classes together, where they met. She was calling me in hopes that I would break up with him, because she had asked him to break up with me, but he refused. She began to plead with me, asking that I break it off with Brian so that the two of them could be together. Again, I just hung up on her. This time I called Natalie to ask her opinion of the situation. She defended Brian, contending that some girl probably had a crush on him and was just angry because I got him first. She encouraged me not to worry about it and to let the phone calls go. When I questioned her about what Gwen had told me, Natalie just blew it off. She thought that what Gwen saw was no big deal, and there was a fine explanation for it. So I decided to shove the feeling of uneasiness down to the pit of my stomach and move on. I tried to act normal with Brian, but the doubt had turned me distant and untrusting.

One evening a few weeks later, I was alone in my dorm room, studying. Brian and I had been arguing lately due to my unease. That night we decided to take some time apart in hopes that the absence would indeed make our hearts grow fonder. As I was sitting at my desk, I got a phone call from Natalie. She was in a panic and told me that I needed to come to "The Reg" as soon as I could; there was something I needed to see. Dread slowly began to rise as my doubt of Brian resurfaced. I knew what I had to see even before I stood to get my purse.

Natalie met me at the door and began to apologize, not wanting to be the one who had to show me the awful scene that I was about to witness. I let the words blur past me as I followed her in a daze. She led me to the back of the bar, where the booths were located. I saw Brian occupying the last booth, leaning forward and talking to some girl who seemed upset. I stood, frozen. My feet felt like lead, for my pain-filled heart had fallen to the floor. Before I could register the image before me, Brian took her hand and led her out of the bar. I heard glass crashing inside my head as my heart shattered.

The rest of the night was spent driving around in Natalie's

Taurus while I utterly broke down. I began to chastise myself for not guarding my heart and for being so completely blind. I feared going back to my dorm room in case Brian was waiting for me there. He did not see me in the bar, but I was certain he would get worried when I was not answering my phone. What in the world was I going to say to him? How could I possibly look him in the eye and see his love for me, which was now tainted? Natalie heard all of my rants and supported me like any friend would in this type of situation. We drove for hours, stopping a few times along the way for junk food and gas. By dawn I was spent, and Natalie took me back to my room, got me settled in, and unplugged my phone before she left.

I spent the next month avoiding Brian, not taking his calls, and guarding my heart when he showed up at my door and pleaded his innocence. He contended that Gwen had called him, asking if he could talk to her friend, who was feeling suicidal. When I inquired about it with Gwen, she denied even knowing the girl except for having seen her in a few classes. I surmised that this was the same girl whom Gwen saw holding Brian's hand in class that one day. I was in hell. Brian was relentless, but I did not know how I was supposed to believe him after all of this. The evidence seemed pretty solid, and I had played the scene at "The Reg" so many times in my head that I was certain of what I saw. I was hurt enough that eventually the awful things I said to Brian finally sent him away, and I was left with trying to figure out how to put the shattered pieces of my heart back together.

It took me several months to begin to even remotely feel like myself again. I had gotten to the point where I could hear our favorite band, Def Leppard, on the radio and not break down in hysterics right there on the spot. I was able to begin to think of our time together with the pain of it only being a dull thud in the background. I still missed Brian. I had not only lost someone for whom I cared deeply, but I had also lost my best friend. Brian and I had gotten along so well; I had felt as though I could share anything with him. That was gone, and I was left with an empty hole in the middle of my chest.

Then one spring afternoon I received a call from Gwen... and Natalie. They left a message giving a detailed account of how they had orchestrated me into believing that Brian had cheated on me. Gwen had lied about the girl in class. Natalie had paid some random girl to call me and tell me that she was Brian's girlfriend. She had also paid that same girl to be at "The Reg" and pretend she was feeling suicidal. Gwen did call Brian and had asked for his help. Once Brian got to the bar, Gwen introduced her "friend" to Brian and then left. The girl had been instructed to get Brian to lead her out by the hand as soon as she saw me. Natalie had given this girl several pictures of Natalie and me together so she would be able to recognize me. And the reason Natalie waited so long to let me in on her "fun little secret"? It was because she wanted to make sure that I had done enough damage to the relationship that Brian would never come back to me. I had. I recalled all the things I had said to him and knew that I would never be able to repair what was broken, not even with the evidence I now had before me. The call ended with the two girls talking and laughing with each other about what a fun time all of it was.

I am not sure how long I stared out my window at the campus or how many times I listened to that message, all the while replaying in my head what Natalie's father had said to me over a year and a half ago. All the hurt and anguish that I had from my relationship came flooding back to me. And it was back with a vengeance; now I also felt the pain and heartbreak over what Natalie had done to me. I thought of her as one of my closest friends. Why? I decided to call her and ask that question. She cackled hysterically and then responded with, "Why? Because I was bored! There is absolutely nothing to do in this God-forsaken town, and I wanted to spice things up a bit." She continued laughing as I slowly hung up the phone. Then the rage came. Rage at her, at Gwen, at that selfish girl who ruined my life for a little extra spending money, and at myself for being such a fool. And then my rage turned toward God. I angrily questioned why He would allow this to happen.

I began screaming at Him as to why He put me in this position. Tears were streaming down my face for the pain that was my life. I was a good girl; I followed God as much as I could. I was not a bad person, so why would God treat me this way? Why should I follow a God who is going to let me get hurt? I had a full-blown temper tantrum in my dorm room, and I expected some answers! I deserved some answers after all I had been through, right?

Instead I received silence.

God never responded to my temper tantrum.

He did not need to. The truth had already been laid out before me through His Word. His Word says, "Come to me, all you who are weary and burdened, and I will give you rest. Take my yoke upon you and learn from me, for I am gentle and humble in heart, and you will find rest for your souls. For my yoke is easy and my burden is light" (Matt. 11:28–30). I just needed to make the choice. I could blame God for what was occurring, or I could stop pitching a fit and seek the truth.

The truth is that there are good among the bad. My friends' choices were not from God. They came out of their free will. So often we forget that, yet God reminds us that bad is going to live among the good. In the parable of the weeds, God talks about how there are weeds among the wheat. Jesus instructs us, "Let both grow together until the harvest. At that time I will tell the harvesters: First collect the weeds and tie them in bundles to be burned; then gather the wheat and bring it into my barn" (Matt. 13:30). Bad things are going to happen to us, but God will take care of us. Just in His time, not ours. The truth, also, was that God was there. The entire time that I pitched my fit, God was in the room. He was just silent. Just as I was with my little girl next to her crib, God was right beside me the whole time. And just as I had to let my little girl go through her tantrum and make her choice, God had to let me make mine.

Did God's heart ache as I was yelling obscenities at Him? Certainly. My heart ached when Marianna was just calling out my name. Did God want to just pick me up and hold me close to Him? Definitely. Would that have been the best thing for me? Definitely not. At that moment I needed to choose. I needed to choose God or find my own reality. And I needed to make that choice on my own. I had all the information laid out before me; I just needed to make a decision based on it. Luckily I chose God that night. He was with me throughout my grieving process and taught me many things in those dark days. However, I had to *let* Him teach me those things.

By sitting next to my daughter's crib and allowing her to throw her tantrum, I let her choose, having all the information laid before her. She knew that I was her mommy, that I would never leave her, and that there was a time and place for everything; it was time for bed.

By God sitting next to me in my dorm and allowing me to throw my tantrum, He let me choose, having all the information laid before me. I knew that He was my Father, that He would never leave me, and that there was a time and place for everything; it was my time to grieve. The truth is that I was wrongly treated, but that was not because of God. And the truth is, God will take care of Natalie's actions one day, but that is not up to me. I do not get to decide what happens to her or when. And I am OK with that now, for He is far better to judge than I.

The truth is also that silence does not mean absence. When God is silent and it seems as if He is not hearing us, it does not mean that He is not there. All of God's interactions with us are in our best interest. So when He is being silent, there is still a lot He is communicating with us. We just need to choose to trust Him and embrace it.

By the end of her tantrum, Marianna had worn herself out; she sighed, laid her head down on the pillow, and let sleep take her into peaceful dreams. By the end of my tantrum, I had also worn myself out; I laid my head on God's lap and let Him take me into a God-filled life.

Chapter

11

❦

Teething With a Vengeance, Hitting the Deadly Dome, Falling Asleep in a Morgue, and God's Tears Mixed in With Ours

———

Marianna's Talk With God

Last night Mari told me that God talked to her. I asked her what He said. She made a heart with her hands and said, "God says He loves us."

I T IS 3:30 a.m., and Marianna has not stopped screaming
since early evening. She is little over a year old, and teething
has come with a vengeance. Her gums are swollen, and she
is running a fever and has diarrhea and night sweats. We have
tried Tylenol, Orajel, and cold, wet rags, and nothing seems to
be taking the edge off. Marianna is starting to get that look of
panic in her eyes and is getting angry with me because I have
not been able to alleviate her agony.

I too begin to panic, wondering when this is ever going to
stop. I have been praying for God to give me some ideas about
how to relieve my daughter's suffering. As I rock my screaming
daughter in my arms, God brings me back to a hot Saturday
summer night four years ago.

Robert and I were living in a sleepy town in Southeastern
Illinois. I was working as a crisis counselor and was on call for
the county hospitals and local police departments. My usual
shift was twenty-four hours a day for four days at a time. It was
a difficult job for me because of all of the darkness that surrounded it: the drug overdoses, suicide attempts, farming acci-
dents, and fatalities. I was even involved in a hostage situation
in which I had to convince a boy to hand his gun over and let
his parents go. One of my most challenging calls out was the
death of a sixteen-year-old high-school student.

School had not been out for long, and the excitement of new-
found freedom was still in the air. Police officers, therapists,
and nurses were discussing when the first fatality might occur,
because somehow, right on the edge of summer, one always did.

It occurred the night I was on call.

Living in the heartland, there is not much for kids to do on
the weekends. Kids have to find their own entertainment, and

it happened to be a bump on an old country gravel road. They nicknamed it "the Deadly Dome" because it could project a car airborne if hit at a high speed, leaving the kids feeling as though they had accomplished something equivalent to Evel Knievel. Everyone around town talked about how dangerous this particular bump was, but somehow it never made it onto the priority list of the highway department.

I received the call around 11:00 p.m. from a nurse at the local emergency room. She informed me that there had been a car accident, one fatality: a fifteen-year-old high school girl. Apparently three girls were out joyriding and decided to go over "the Deadly Dome." The three girls hit the bump at high speed, careening the car toward the ditch and hitting a telephone pole before landing. It catapulted one girl who was not wearing her seat belt out into the cornfield.

She was killed instantly.

I remember being called to go to the hospital to inform the mother that her daughter had been killed and to provide her comfort. That is no small feat. How do you provide comfort to someone who has just lost a child? I was not a parent at that time, so it was even harder for me to wrap my head around the thoughts and feelings of someone who had lost her child so tragically. On the entire way to the hospital, I prayed that God would provide me with words of wisdom, words that would take the pain away.

Nothing came to mind.

I had no clue what I was going to do once I got there. I felt as if I might puke. I walked through the sliding-glass doors; the bright fluorescent lights blinded me, and a blast of cold air hit me, making me shiver. What also hit me were the murmuring sounds of grief. It seemed as though the entire high school had come to grieve this horrific loss. I immersed myself into the crowd, giving words of comfort as I passed people, searching for the parents. I finally found the mother sitting in a private room with one of the nurses. No father was present. As I entered, the nurse was in the midst of telling her that she needed to identify the body. The nurse introduced me and informed her that I would be the one to go with her when she felt ready to go to the morgue. Upon that last statement, the nurse quietly and quickly left, leaving me alone to handle the information she had just given. *Are you kidding me? I have to be the one to take her to the morgue? Isn't that the job of the doctor or the morgue guy?* I certainly was not prepared for this, nor do I remember receiving training in this particular area. But I was in it now, no turning back. I took a deep breath, said a short, demanding prayer that God be with me, and headed toward the couch.

I sat on the couch and sidled up beside this grief-stricken mother. She looked directly into my eyes, searching for answers. I had none. The only thing I could find myself to do was to put my arm around her. She sank into my shoulders and sobbed. She sobbed that gut-wrenching, soul-ripping, heart-broken sob that comes from deep within your being. I continued to beg for God to give me some answers, to give me some words to carry her through this time of trial. Still I received continued silence.

Even when it was time to take her to the morgue to identify her daughter, I continued to receive no signs of how to comfort this woman. We walked with our arms clasped tightly around one another; she was sobbing, and I was praying. We rounded the corner and entered the room where her daughter lay, and the mother fell to the floor. I fell with her and found myself crying with her while I held her in my arms and rocked her.

I'm not sure how long we stayed like that; it seemed like hours. I was lost in those moments with her, immersed within the realm of grief. I remember the sobbing tapering off and her feeling slack in my arms. I looked to find that she had dozed off on me in that cold, sterile room just a few feet from her deceased daughter. When she awoke a few minutes later, we made our way back down the hall to the nurses' station. She told the doctor that the girl in the morgue was indeed her daughter and that she was ready to go home. She hugged me tightly—gratefully, it seemed—kissed me on the cheek, and went out into the night to face her future.

I drove home feeling deeply saddened, confused, and uncomprehending. *Why didn't God provide me with some answers for her? Why did He just leave me hanging to deal with it by myself?* I knew that God had a plan and that He had some reasons for all this grief and loss that had befallen so many people. I could not comprehend why He refused to share it with me.

I continued not to comprehend until about a month ago. It was the middle of the night, and Marianna was screaming in pain. She not only was teething but also had a bellyache. We gave her medicine to try and provide comfort, but until the medicine kicked in, our little girl was in some serious hurt! I held her in my arms, rocked her, sang to her, and just let her know that I loved her. Between screams she would look at me, not comprehending what was going on and why Mommy was not taking the pain away.

Now, our daughter was only thirteen months old at the time, so her ability to understand complex things was limited. I could not explain to her that she was in pain because her molars were working their way through her gums, which is a painful process. I could not explain that her tummy was cramping up because she had one too many pieces of popcorn with Daddy before bedtime. There was a reason why this was happening to her, as well as a reason for her pain. Her mind just was not developed enough to wrap her head around these explanations. So the best thing I could do was to comfort her by holding her close to me. And that proved to be enough for her. Her teeth were still hurting and her belly was still cramping, but she was able to rest her head upon my shoulder, stop crying, and find relief in my arms.

As I sat in the rocker with her, my mind wandered back to that fateful night described above. There was no way I could have given that mother answers because she would not have been able to comprehend what I was saying. Our minds are so limited compared to God and His ways. There would have been no way for me to understand it well enough to explain it to her, let alone for her to be able to comprehend why her daughter was taken. God's plan is so vast and beyond our recognition that there are no answers for us that we could take in and understand. Just like my daughter, our minds are young when it comes to the comprehending of God's plan. In times when we do not understand and are searching for answers, the best thing God can do for us is to hold us in His arms. The best that we can do is to accept His embrace and have faith that God is taking care of us. God knows that in those moments, it is not answers we need but the embrace. God drifts with us on our waves of grief. We just need to let Him silently guide us home.

Going home that fatal summer night, I felt like a failure for being unable to give her the answers she wanted. Sitting in my rocker years later, I realized that I had succeeded because I was able to give her what she needed. God's love poured out to her through me. Through love, comfort, and being with her through that experience (at least for a little while), I was able to give her what she needed. That is what her hug and kiss were communicating to me. She was ready to go home because she had gotten what she needed. Her well had been filled up enough to carry her at least through to the next phase that she would encounter. I did not speak one word to her the entire time I was with her, but what I did spoke volumes.

Garth Brooks has a song titled "Unanswered Prayers" that talks about God not answering our prayers and how that is a blessing. However, I do not believe that there are prayers that go unanswered. For God's silence sometimes *is* the answer.

God answered my prayers through silence because He was telling me that silence was, indeed, the answer. Most often I find that God answers in a totally different direction from what I expect. When I pray, I already have a preconceived notion of what answer I should receive in return, only to have God blow it to pieces and take me in a completely new direction.

We may not know why things happen or what God's plan in all of this is. We can take rest in that receiving silence from God when we are searching for those answers is not because He is not answering.

It is because His arms are wrapped around us, His tears mixed in with ours, sharing in our grief.

12

Heavy Summer Air,
Sinking in a Couch,
Amazing Plans and Mess-ups, and
Mere Reflections on a Quiet Monitor

Favorite Thing to Do

One day I asked Marianna what she thought Jesus's favorite thing to do was. Without hesitation she said, "To be with us."

ONE EVENING I was rocking Marianna at my parents' house. It was a hot, sweltering, midsummer evening in the Midwest, an evening in which the air was so heavy and laden with humidity that it seemed smothering. I took Marianna into the bedroom with air conditioning, and she lay on me and drank her bottle as she was settling down for the night. She had had a big day on the farm and was tired and needed rest; however, when her bottle was empty, all she could do was wallow around on my lap. She would stay in one position for a few minutes only to move to another and then another. I patted and rubbed her back while singing to her. I could tell by her movements that she just was not allowing herself to let the day go. She was so excited to be on the farm that she didn't want it to end, even if only for a few hours. She thought that she might be missing out on something and that I was keeping her from it because I wanted her to go to sleep. No matter how I reasoned with her that that was not the case, she continued to fight me.

I finally just whispered in her ear that I loved her and wanted what was best for her, which was to rest for a while. I promised her that everything was taken care of and even more amazing things were planned for tomorrow. I asked her to just trust the promises I made and know that I would take care of her. After stating this mantra over and over again, my baby finally let go and let me envelop her in my arms. Once she let go, she was able to sink into a deep, peaceful sleep that lasted for the next twelve hours.

Later that night when it was my bedtime, I found that I too was fighting sleep. Thoughts were drifting to everything that needed to get done once we returned home: how we were

going to pay for a broken kitchen sink, whether we would have
enough from my paycheck to help pay the bills, and how I was
going to heal a relationship that needed mending.

Once my mind grew tired of using actual words and sen-
tences, I was able to hear God whispering in my ear. This is
what He said:

"I love you." (See John 3:16.)

"You need to rest awhile." (See Matthew 11:28.)

"I have taken care of things." (See Acts 14:17.)

"Stop worrying, because I have amazing plans for
you." (See Matthew 6:25.)

"You are taken care of, My child." (See Psalm 36:7.)

I too found myself drifting off to this soothing rhythm of
God, which ended in a peaceful sleep.

Tonight I am sitting in my living room, listening to the
monitor as Robert is putting our daughter to bed. It is her bedtime, yet once again she is fighting sleep. As I type this, I can
hear her crying over the monitor and Robert trying to console
her by talking softly and patting her. She is refusing to take
his comfort, continuing to scream, and fighting against what
is good for her.

I begin to send thoughts up to her, letting her know that we
love her, that she needs rest, and that Daddy and I will take
care of her. I offer this mantra up as a prayer and ask that she
will allow Robert to comfort her and lead her in the direction that she needs to go. I begin to dance to this cadence, and
Marianna must feel this dance, for she finally decides to dance
into sleep.

After a little while I sink into the couch and just close my
eyes. Soon I hear God's whisperings:

"I love you."

"You need to rest awhile."

"I have taken care of things."

"Stop worrying because I have amazing plans for you."

"You are taken care of, My child."

He repeats my words back to me once again and makes me realize that I am made in His image. I am a mere reflection of who He is. I have such an intense and fierce love for Marianna and only want the best for her. If she were being harmed, I would be a mama bear and fight tooth and nail to free her. Yet, as intense, wild, and passionate as I am about my daughter, my maternal instincts are a mere glimpse of how God feels for us.

Why is it so hard for us to just let ourselves go and let God take care of us? We get frustrated with our children when they fight against us, yet we continuously do it with our own heavenly Father. I think back on the passage, "Then little children were brought to Jesus for him to place his hands on them and pray for them. But the disciples rebuked those who brought them. Jesus said, 'Let the little children come to me, and do not hinder them, for the kingdom of heaven belongs to such as these'" (Matt. 19:13–14).

In eating of the tree of the knowledge of good and evil, our innocence was taken. It opened our eyes and made us no longer children; therefore, in our relationship with God, I think we sometimes forget that that is exactly who we are. We are children in need of guidance, nurturance, love, acceptance, truth, safety, and someone whom we can fully trust. Marianna had no reason not to trust in me, and she still fought against me. We have absolutely no reason not to trust God, yet we do this on a daily basis. God tells us to go in one direction because He knows it is good for us, only to have us do the exact opposite, refusing Him so that we can do it on our own. God knows that, if left to our own devices, we will mess it up, just as I know that if left up to our daughter, she would mess up her night of sleep and schedule.

Just as I ache for Marianna to trust and follow me, I believe it is similar with God. He is aching for the times when we will follow Him and give in to His comfort and His direction. I believe He is constantly whispering in our ear to follow Him and that all will be good.

And it will be. Hasn't He shown you that time and time again? I think about all the times in which I have given up and followed God. Every time I have, the path has worked out perfectly. Maybe not to *my* perfection but certainly perfectly in line with God's will. God invited us to start a family, and by following Him we received the best gift in the world—our daughter. We also have in the past chosen not to follow God and the conclusion wasn't so stellar. I can remember the time my husband decided to take a job that he thought would be easier and offer more opportunity than the job he was currently working. In Robert's prayer time, God had told him not to take the job. He quit the company where he had worked ten years to take this new job. About a month into it, he realized that the president of the corporation was shifting business money into her personal account. He reported her to one of the board members, who he later found out was related to her. He was ultimately fired over the incident, leaving him jobless with a new mortgage payment. Our mess-ups were always when we did not follow God, never when we did.

Knowing how much easier it is to just follow Christ and to trust in those who have your best interest at heart, I look at my child in frustration during the times when she fights sleep. I think to myself, *Why won't you just listen to me? I know what is best and right for you!* I can imagine God thinking the same thing about us. Romans 8:28 tells us, "And we know that in all things God works for the good of those who love him, who have been called according to his purpose." Over and over again He proves to us that He has our best interest at heart. Over and over again He proves to us that He is trustworthy and has planned only good for us. It would be so easy for my little girl and for the rest of the family if she just followed our lead. It could also be so easy for us if we were to follow God's lead; yet so often we do not. (I am not saying that God's way is an easy way of life, but I am saying that His ways are good and perfect according to His plan.)

God opened my eyes to knowing that I am no different from my daughter when it comes to my relationship with Him. I am a child in need of a Father who is fully present and whom I can trust to make the right decisions for me. I am too young in this fallen body and spirit to ever be able to take care of myself or know better than God.

As my thoughts power down, I realize that the monitor is now quiet. I can hear only the rocking of the recliner and the soft whisperings of my husband's voice. Our little girl has finally taken rest in his arms, and all is right with the world.

13

Sighing the Little-Kid Sigh, No Need to Pray Any Longer, Unworthiness Baked Right in, and Amazing Tutelage

---

Marianna's Take on Her Mother

Late at night Mari says, "Mom, you know what's special about you? Your heart. Your happy heart."

M Y FAMILY AND I spent a week in Michigan at a cabin. Our cabin sat on a point, surrounded by water on three sides. Every window in the cabin looked out over the water, and it was one of the most peaceful places I had ever been. Our vacation was not about packing in as many activities as possible or showing Marianna everything there was to see in terms of fun. Our vacation was about spending quality family time together, rejuvenating, and coming to know God better than we have before. A few times during the trip I was able to be by myself while my husband and daughter were elsewhere. Otherwise we spent most of our waking moments together, loving each other, spending time together, relaxing, and enjoying ourselves together. All the while God was dancing among us. The week was special in that we had days of meandering, exploring, resting, and playing. However, I remember one night as being extra special.

Early in the evening, Robert had built a campfire. Marianna is a barefoot girl; she loves to be barefoot. However, it was muddy near the campfire, so we asked Marianna to keep her shoes on. She proceeded to untie one shoe. We continued to ask her to keep her shoes on. Finally she said, "What? I can't hear you over the 'moke!" After a good laugh, we made sure Marianna heard us the next time and settled into the campfire. We made s'mores, watched swans and boaters drift by, told stories, and sang songs. As the stars came out, Marianna crawled into my lap and said that she wanted to snuggle with me. These are my favorite moments with my daughter. She was at peace in my arms and tucked safely into me. All was right with the world in those moments. Robert started to read Psalm 119 while Marianna and I sat quietly listening. The psalmist talked about seeking the heart of the Lord and keeping His laws and statutes. He talked about how wonderful it is to walk with the Lord and to seek the Lord's will.

My mind wandered to Marianna.

I looked down upon my daughter and quickly saw all the reasons why I was in love with her—her big brown eyes catching the light of the fire; her hand absent-mindedly stroking my arm; her way of sighing that little-kid sigh when she is finally relaxing.

I am reminded that I had never laughed so much—or so hard—before I had her, how every day I cannot wait for her to open her eyes and tell me, "Mom, it's a beautiful day!" or how she runs in a funny little way when she gets excited. My heart is overflowed with joy, peace, laughter, and love because of this precious gift that God has given me. I do not know what I would do without her. My purpose feels more complete now that she is here. I feel absolutely privileged to be her mom and am thankful every day for her existence in my life.

This is the story of how Marianna came to be.

Robert and I purchased our old Victorian house in 2004. We were what people called "DINKs," or "Double Income, No Kids." We were both working full-time as therapists, and we spent the rest of our time making the house our own. By the spring of the following year we had finished all the rooms except for the back bedroom and what was deemed "the parlor room" in the front of the house. We decided to turn the back bedroom into a nursery even though we had no intention of starting a family anytime soon. We spent the next four and a half months in the nursery making a collage of the *Peanuts* characters; you know, Charlie Brown, Linus, Lucy, etc. Above the crib we painted Linus and Snoopy sleeping next to each other. We painted Schroeder playing his piano, Sally sitting at a school desk, and Lucy missing a catch in her baseball uniform. We filled the room with pictures of all the things our future baby could be or do. There's a picture of Sally crying as

Linus tells her he is not her Sweet Baboo because we knew our child would get hurt; there's a picture of Pig Pen in all of his muddy glory because we knew our child would get muddy. The room was filled with loving pictures like these, and it was done out of full-blown love even without a clue as to whether a child was in our future.

Robert's Nan, however, was certain that there was a child in our future. Nan was Robert's ninety-six-year-old paternal grandmother. Nan was Polish and came over to the States when she was just a little girl; however, she still had the thickest accent. When I met her, she was in her mid-nineties and still living with her husband, Pop, in the house in which she grew up. Nan and Pop were tough old birds who absolutely adored and loved each other. They were the type of people who worked hard, played hard, and enjoyed every bit of life that was given to them.

Whenever we were home, we would go to visit Nan and Pop. Pop was hard of hearing, and so he would sit quietly while Nan carried the conversation, which mostly drifted to the subject of kids. She was adamant that we needed to start a family and that she wanted to see a great-grandchild before God took her. At the time we knew we were not ready but tried to let her down gently by saying that it was not the right time. She scoffed at that and was determined that we had a family. God love her! Nan never got a chance to meet Marianna here on Earth, but I do believe she might have known her before we did.

God gave us the vision to start a family while making the nursery. I can remember sitting on the floor in the nursery many times and praying to God that I would get pregnant and fulfill His plan for us. I would sit for hours, dreaming of the child who would grow up in that room. That room represented God's promise, much like the rainbow. Whenever I would feel doubt about having a child, I only had to walk into that room, and I knew that it would be filled one day.

Two months after hearing from God, I became pregnant. Robert and I made trips back home to alert our families. A few weeks before I found out, Nan passed away, and Pop followed her only a week later. Robert and I were saddened that Nan was not with us to hear the news; that was until we got our own news from Robert's mom. When we broke the news to Robert's parents, they, of course, were delighted; his mom, Verla, however, acted as though she had already known. She just quietly sat back with a smile slowly coming across her face. When we inquired about it, this is what she told us:

> Well, I've known how Nan has always bugged you two about starting a family. It would almost irritate her when you would visit, only to be told again that you two weren't ready. A week before she died, I was over there visiting her. She told me that we didn't have to pray any longer for God to give you guys a child. He told her that He had already sent one to you.

We were blown away! We quickly did the math, and I was two weeks pregnant when Nan had made that phone call. We knew then that Marianna would be named after her.

When it was time for Marianna to be born, I went to the hospital on a Monday evening to be induced. A nurse, Sheila, was with me for the evening shift and left at 10:00 p.m. As she left, she stated that if I had not given birth by 7:00 a.m., she would see me tomorrow morning. I labored the entire night, and when 7:00 a.m. rolled around? Still no baby girl. There was no Sheila either. She finally came in about a half an hour late, explaining that she about could not make it on time due to the horrible storm above the hospital. She said that the lightning and thundering were so fierce that they stopped traffic. Marianna was born three hours later. Five minutes after her birth, the storm ceased and the sun shone. Sheila could not believe her eyes. She went to the window and opened the curtains wide to let the sun shine in. We knew what to do at that moment. In honor of God we chose Marianna's middle name to be Thunder, for God had spoken through thunder regarding her birth.

So that was how Marianna Thunder came to be in our lives. It has been such a wondrous and joyous adventure. Yet, amidst the joy and beauty of it all, my mind wanders to darkness at times. What if we had not listened to God? What if we had blown off His will for us to start a family? What if I had not felt ready or had thought that God had wrongly estimated that it was the right time? If I had not been in line with God's will and chose a different path, I would have missed out on such a precious gift; I would not have Marianna. Just the mere thought of it crushes my heart. Yet how many times have I ignored God in other things? What other precious gifts did I miss out on because I did not diligently follow His will? I think many of us would have crushed hearts if we knew how many wonderful gifts we pass up each day that we are not diligently seeking God's will. Maybe we are trying to seek His will but just not doing it properly.

As I examine my own life, I find that I pray, but my prayers are often narrow-minded, meek, and selfish. As I offer words up to God, they are often plans about how I think things should go in my life. They are requests for how I think God should deal with problems that arise. My prayers often do not seek out His will, look for His say on the matter, and ask for His will to be done. Oh, I finish every prayer with "Your will be done," but is that *truly* what my heart is saying? More often than not, when I say, "Your will be done," what I really mean is, "Your will be done as long as it is my will and as long as it is carried out in the way that I see fit." Is that true submission? I highly doubt it.

When I look at my precious daughter lying in my arms like an angel, my mind then has to wonder why on earth wouldn't

I allow God to handle everything for me, for He gave me her. When I look at all the things that God has provided for me, it has been far above the standards that I would have achieved by myself: my husband, my daughter, my home, my occupation... I could go on and on. When I look at all the things I have tried to achieve myself and all the decisions I have made without His divine direction, I cringe at the results. I am ashamed and mortified at the outcomes of some of my behaviors.

Growing up, I often felt scared, lonely, and unloved. I can't quite pinpoint when or how that occurred. Instead I think it was a gradual mixture of ingredients that baked into me unworthiness that I could not peel off. People often think that children with low self-esteem like mine do not know God, but I did. My family went to church every Sunday. I attended Sunday school, vacation Bible school, and a Christian camp. I knew God and what He was about yet still felt unloved. The church taught me about being a sinner, not being a loved child of God. It taught me that I was bad and would never measure up to what God had in mind. The church I attended did not talk much about the love of God or His mercy. Between that and the crux of my family's dynamics in which I lived, I felt utterly alone and desperate.

That is why I began to steal. I wanted something to fill the void that was inside me. I also wanted someone to see me because I felt invisible. My grandmother had loads of jewelry, so when I went to visit her and my grandfather, I would take a necklace or a bracelet. My grandmother never paid much attention to me, and this was—in my own weird little way—a way of connecting with her. I had something that she loved, which made me love it. Feeling a mutual love for an object allowed me to feel emotionally close to her. I did not feel love directly from her but could feel her love through this object that she so adored.

I would take the item home and fantasize that she had

thrown a party for me and the piece of jewelry was a present that she had made especially for me. The item would be lavishly wrapped and presented to me with honor. My grandmother would present it to me in front of our entire family and give abundant praise and adoration for me. Upon opening it, everyone would clap and give me countless praise for being such a wonderful little girl who deserved such a prize.

I would also fantasize that when my family found out that I had stolen these things (for I knew it would happen at some point), they would understand my reasons and get down on their hands and knees, asking for my forgiveness for forgetting about me. They would allow me to keep the items and would promise to never forget about me and to love me the way that I needed them to.

Of course, none of those things ever happened. What did happen was lots of disappointing statements and being grounded, being forced to give the things back and apologize, and threats of being sent away if I could not "straighten up." I felt lonelier, more powerless, and even more unloved. I had felt invisible before, but this was the first time that I wished that I actually was! I sunk deeper within myself and felt I had nowhere to go. I retreated into myself and into my room. I read, played, and kept myself occupied. I did anything to keep my mind away from thinking about what an awful, unlovable child I felt I was.

One night the sorrow became too much, and I began to sob. I sobbed so hard that my chest hurt, and my face turned splotchy and red with rash. It was the uncontrollable sobbing that comes from a long time of pent-up hurt, sadness, and resentment residing in my body and finally needing to be released. After what seemed like hours, my crying had abated, and I was able to start breathing regularly again. My mind began to clear from the fog of sadness; at that moment, God decided to show up.

God shared His love with me and began to talk to me about His plan for me. I could feel His arms wrap around me, and peace consumed me. I no longer felt scared or alone. I felt complete for the first time since I could remember, and it was a feeling I did not want to let go anytime soon. When God asked me to follow Him that night, I readily agreed. When I made the agreement, I did not know—nor would I for many years to come—exactly what that would mean; however, I knew it was my only good option.

That night was the beginning of a long journey of trials and tribulations in following God. It was difficult to change my life; my circumstances and environment hadn't changed. I had to learn how to act differently within the same situations in which I had previously been. I do not believe it can happen overnight. At least it didn't for me, and I think it is that way with most people. Everything is a process; I think it has to be in order for us to learn everything there is to learn and to embody true change.

Robert and I are huge fans of the show *So You Think You Can Dance.* It is a competition show among dancers. There are contemporary dancers, hip-hop dancers, ballroom, crump, etc. It starts with the auditions, carries through competition and voting, and ends with the finale, when the final two dance their butts off for the title. They take incredible dancers and push them beyond their limits to make them beyond incredible by the time the finale airs. The dancers get pushed and prodded beyond even what they believe they can do. Some quit, some become injured, and some are asked to leave for more training before they can compete. It is a process. I think that this is a great illustration of what our journey is like with God.

We are fabulously and wonderfully made by God. We have the freewill to follow God and be under His tutelage. If we agree to allow God to provide us guidance in the walk with

Christ, then we are going to be sent through the training process. He will teach us how to transcend the hardships, heartaches, and pains to become even more fabulous and incredible. That is no easy feat, and I believe that is why only a few actually make it.

I am in the middle of my journey and feel that I have learned and am learning so much. I also feel that I have quite a long way to go. However, God has blessed me through this journey. I am far from that scared, lonely little girl to the point in which I sometimes do not even recognize that that person used to be me. Through following God, I feel loved, complete, special, and whole. The feelings that I was trying to obtain by stealing could only be obtained through the acceptance of God. I am learning that all good things can only be obtained through Christ. I am at the point in my journey where I recognize my blessings, and that just makes me love God all the more and makes me desire to follow and worship Him even more.

In his book *the Path of Celtic Prayer: An Ancient Way to Everyday Joy*, Calvin Miller talks about how the ancient Celts thought that praying ceaselessly meant that every thought, desire, feeling, and behavior were offered up to God as prayer. Thus, prayer became not only a communication with God but also an act of worship as well. Every ounce of them could be offered up as a prayer of worship to God; with that being their focus, they were always looking to God and seeking out His will versus their own selfish wants and desires.[1]

This is where I am currently at in this journey of mine. I am learning how every thought, desire, behavior, and feeling of mine can be offered up as a prayer to God and in turn become an act of worship. I am beginning to focus upward rather than inward; dying to myself rather than asking God to live through my wants.

And so, as I look down at my child sleeping in my arms,

I pull her closer to me and kiss her repeatedly on the forehead. In doing so I am offering up a prayer of thanks to the One who made her. I worship the One who gave me such an incredible gift in the midst of my amazing journey with God.

Chapter

14

Backwashing a Pool in a Diaper,
the Sound of "Orry,"
Being Best at Bad, and
Forgiving Toward Harmony

The Dancing Trinity

One night during the *Tinker Bell* movie credits, Marianna, Robert, and I were dancing in the living room. We were twirling, leaping, and flowing with each other and through each other. Our energy flowed past one another in pure light.

Do you ever wonder if the Trinity dances with us in such ways?

I T WAS A normal, lovely, spring afternoon. The air was crisp yet inviting, so Marianna and I decided to enjoy it in the backyard. I wanted to work on the pool to get it in better shape for when Robert came home, so I began to backwash it. I had the pool-house door open for the hose to run out into the yard, and the mechanics of the pump were exposed. My little one decided that she needed to help Mom by turning the switch to the pump off and on. I was across the pool near the filter and was not close enough to pull her away, so I said, "No," and told her to back up. Being almost two and deathly defiant, she continued to play with the switch. After three chances, I walked over, told her no, and then for effect swatted her diaper-padded butt once.

Several emotions flashed across her face: surprise, confusion, shock, and, most of all, hurt. Tears welled up in her eyes, and her little mouth started to frown and quiver. Her breath hitched once or twice before she leapt into my arms and held me tight, whispering, "Orry." At that moment I just hugged her and whispered in her ear how much I loved and adored her. The need to punish and teach a lesson fled from me quickly and was replaced by my need to let her know how much she was loved. I continued to hold her, rock her, and whisper my love to her. After a while she gripped my face between her two little hands, looked me directly in the face, and asked, "Otay?" I smiled and responded by gripping her little head in my hands and saying, "You and me, we're OK. We're good, and I love you." It took a brief moment for understanding to reach her, and when it did, a smile began at her mouth and ended in her eyes. Her entire face lit up like a Christmas tree, and she knew.

She knew that no matter what negative behavior she might have engaged in, she was still loved and adored.

In that moment, I understood the forgiveness of God. The moment we look up at God with full repentance in our heart, all is forgotten. He picks us up and hugs us tightly while whispering, "I love and adore you, My child." (How great is that love?) No matter what our actions are, He focuses on the relationship. He focuses not on our behavior but on *who* we are, His children. My husband and I love Marianna with all of our hearts, and no matter what she chooses to do, we will always love and adore her immensely. Yet no matter how intense our feelings toward her are, they are meek in comparison with God's feelings for us. I think back to how we are made in His image, meaning that we are just a mere reflection of who God is. I would have died if it meant making Marianna feel loved and adored again, yet that is exactly what God did to show us how much He loves and adores us.

It is not forgiveness we need, for we are already forgiven. Colossians 2:13–14 states, "When you were dead in your sins and in the uncircumcision of your sinful nature, God made you alive with Christ. *He forgave us all our sins*, having canceled the written code, with its regulations, that was against us and that stood opposed to us; he took it away, nailing it to the cross" (emphasis added). The Holy Spirit says in Hebrews 10:17, "Their sins and lawless acts I will remember no more." If our sins are forgiven, then why do we need to confess and repent? With forgiveness from the Father already given, our confessions and repentance just allow us to deepen our relationships with God. Confession brings about freedom. It brings freedom from our thoughts and actions and allows us to release that which is holding us captive. It permits us to open ourselves up and bring in more love, peace, and joy. It allows for intimacy and a closeness that we would not have if we did not state our wrongs to Him. How wonderful. How wonderful to have a God who no longer keeps track of our sins but just yearns to have a deeper relationship with us.

It was a normal, sunny, Midwestern summer, yet in the normalcy of it all, a miracle occurred. The miracle was learning about God's love through my relationship with my daughter. To me, it was not only a lesson about God's love but about learning that my husband and I were on the right track in parenting her. We focused on the relationship we had with Marianna versus what she did and did not do. So many parents say that they love their child no matter what, yet they focus on their behavior rather than their identity. I see this so often in the counseling realm. Yet God's way is about the relationship and who that person is.

So often I see parents disciplining their children by telling them that they are bad for what they did. I hear them focus on their bad behaviors being tied to who they are rather than what they have done. This can be very damaging to one's soul because they then get the message that *they* are inherently bad, not their choices. This is how feelings of low self-esteem and worthlessness begin to develop in children. We need to make a conscious distinction between their behavior and identity.

In the story of the fall of man, when God confronted Adam for eating from the tree of the knowledge of good and evil, He asked, "What have you *done?*" (Gen. 3:13, KJV, emphasis added). God named their wrong behavior rather than who they were as people. He never told Adam and Eve that they were sinful, bad people. He clearly stated to Adam, "Because you listened to your wife and ate from the tree about which I commanded you..." (Gen. 3:17). He specifically told Adam why he was receiving the consequences and clearly showed that it had to do with the choices he made, not because of who he was as a person.

I believe that this is where we have gone wrong in many respects. Many churches and Christians like to call out the person as being sinful, wrong, or bad rather than *behavior* in which the person has engaged. When you separate the two, much healing and understanding can be given. There is hope that the person can change. I see so many kids in my office who are devoid of hope. The reason for this is because they feel that they were born evil or are inherently bad. How is there room for change or growth when this stunted viewpoint has been given about them?

I was working with a seventeen-year-old boy who had sexually molested several children in his mom's day care. He was in our last-chance program, which meant that this was his last stop. If he did not complete this program, he would be heading to the Department of Corrections. During one of our sessions, we were talking about why he had molested so many children. He responded, "Ya know, Miss Monique, if you were told your whole life that you were nothing, that you were a bad kid, that you were meant for evil...how could you be good? There wasn't nothing else for me to do but be bad. I worked my butt off becoming the best at it. At least then I could be the best at somethin'."

If God had called Adam and Eve evil or bad and cursed them instead of their behavior, where would that have left them? They would have had no place to go. They would have had no choice but to be evil and do evil acts. God even addressed Satan in this same manner. He said to the serpent in Genesis 3:14, "Because you have *done* this" (emphasis added). He even focused on how Satan behaved rather than who he intrinsically was.

If we want our children to grow up knowing who they are in Christ and feeling secure about it, then we need to separate their behaviors from who they are. Because of the fall of man, these are two very different things and need to be treated as such. I know that I stumble as a parent and that there are probably ways in which I will mess up my daughter; however, this will not be one of them. She is only a toddler, but she very clearly knows that there is a difference between what she does and who she fundamentally is. This will allow her to grow in the ways that God has intended and will give her freedom to choose correctly as she goes through her journey of life.

May we see the people whom God created in ourselves and others. May we see more than just our behaviors and forgive easily those who may have wronged us. In doing so, we move toward deeper relationships with those who wronged us as well as with our Lord. May we choose to bring about more harmony to the chaos of our world through forgiveness.

Chapter

15

Theater for Cows,
Work Trumps Food,
Smack-Dab Living, and
Awkward Somersaults

Little Toes

Robert and Marianna were talking about how God made her. She threw her bare foot into his lap and said, "Why did Jesus make my lil' toe crooked? Is it because He's funny? He likes jokes. That silly Jesus!"

Marianna thinks Jesus made her toe crooked because He has a sense of humor.

I GREW UP ON a farm about fifty miles south of Chicago. The closest town census was at eleven hundred, while I had a whopping twenty-two kids in my high-school graduating class. Needless to say, I grew up in the country of a small Midwestern town. My parents had Angus beef cattle, a pond, and quite a few acres of farmland than ran alongside a creek (which should be pronounced "crik," the way all the locals call it). I spent many hours in the barn, talking and entertaining the cows as well as exploring that old creek with the water slowly trickling to only God knows where. I loved growing up on that land. That was where I found God. I took many trips alone to the creek or the grasslands nearby. I talked with God often as I picked flowers, looked at bugs, and wondered how such a humongous tree could have grown in such a shallow piece of land beside the creek bed. It was quiet enough for me to hear God and to learn how He created me to be. I love that old piece of land. It not only stores my history but also the history of my ancestors as it has been passed down generation to generation. Its rhythm coincides with my heartbeat, and I know that I belong.

In regard to my family, however, it was a different story. Among my parents and older brother, I always felt as if I were adopted. I did not understand them, nor they, me; that was why I pretty much kept to myself most days. I wandered the land, made up theatrical stories and plays to act out to the cows, and read many books of faraway lands and hauntingly beautiful characters. I had read the entire Bible by the age of eight and fell in love with it, not understanding yet what it was that I had just fallen in love with. My dad worked constantly, and my mother loved cooking in the kitchen, but they never quite loved having help around, and my brother was off working on some other farmer's land. But this story is about my dad, so I will start with him.

My father was one of eight kids in a Catholic household. His own father was a farmer by trade. He grew up poor and uneducated; he left school early on in order to help the family. He never had his own toys or his own clothes. He often went to bed hungry and woke up to no breakfast because the work had to be done, and there simply was not anything to eat. A hunger burned in my dad that led him to become extremely successful in life. He did not want his taste of childhood to remain in adulthood, so he earned his GED, took a job at a huge electric company, and worked his butt off. Every time a storm hit, he was out there. Every time a heat wave took out the electricity, he was on the move, getting it fixed. When he was not at work, he was in the fields or the barn. I never saw my dad in the morning, for he went off to work hours before I even woke up for school. In the spring and summer there were many nights when I saw him at dinner but not after because he was back out in the field until way past my bedtime. He wanted to make sure that he provided for his kids. And he did. We had a nice house, a plethora of food and drink, and a closet full of clothes, toys, and books. However, we never just had Dad. We were never provided with him, and he was what we needed more than any of those other things.

My brother grew up angry at my father, whereas I had more of a daughter's understanding toward him. I knew where he came from and why he was a workaholic. I knew that his paycheck represented the words "I love you," his long hours away from home represented "I am here for you," and his constant drive to be doing something to earn money represented "I want better for you than what I had." But that does not mean I was not hurt by it. So many fathers today believe that if they provide money and stuff for their children, they

119

are showing their children love. That is not the case. Children just want their fathers. Period. They would rather forgo those things—the vacations and the dance and music lessons—to have one-on-one time with their dads. I hear this all the time from teenagers in private therapeutic sessions as they explain why they are estranged from their fathers. I also know it because I was one of those kids. I would rather have forgone the clothes, toys, and books to have him to come to one of my volleyball games or do somersaults with me in the yard. Yet back then, my father could not have done any of those things for he became a product of his environment versus the person who God created him to be. I understand that now, but even with a child's understanding there are wounds that bleed even today.

I am now thirty-seven years old and live in an old Victorian house, smack-dab in the middle of town. This, again, is all God's doing because I would prefer a house out in the country from which I could see no other houses, just trees, farmland, and maybe a little babbling brook or creek. If we did, however, live in an area like I just described, we would not be able to reach the countless number of people that we do where we are living. Although I am grateful for this house and the opportunities I get to serve God, I am saddened that my little girl does not get to experience the peaceful, quiet country life that I so much adored.

Every summer my husband and I make it a point to get Marianna out to the farm (which is about three and a half hours away) as much as possible. As so often happens with age, my parents have changed a bit. They love spending time with our daughter. When Marianna was just a baby, Robert and I had a wonderful conversation with my parents. When I told my dad how I felt growing up and having him gone most of the time, Dad said, "I regret things I did while you were growing up." It gave me hope that things might be a little different with Marianna because of what came out of that talk. So we make sure Marianna gets out to the farm for three or four days at a time. She gets up early and helps my dad do chores in the barn; she helps my parents plant and water the flowers; she and my dad will sit for long periods and fish by the dock of the pond, only to throw the fish back immediately after they are caught on their hooks. They ride on the Gator through the trees, look for baby bunnies, and swing on the playground that my parents have slowly put together in the backyard for their three grandkids. Marianna is so busy with them that she never gets a nap in; she sleeps constantly once she is back home with us to rest up from all that she has done. She is constantly in my father's—"Papa" to her—back pocket. For days after she arrives home, all we hear is, "Papa and I . . ." She absolutely adores my dad and cannot wait to get back to the farm to do it all over again with him.

One week I decided to go with her to the farm. I needed a little getaway and wanted the peace and solace of the farm for a while. I slept in and had time to read and do all the things I don't normally get to do with a toddler around, since she was constantly with my dad. School was still in session at that time, so my mother was still working as a teacher's aide. My father decided to help someone at a job site on the day that we were planning to leave, so we said good-bye to him the night before because we figured we would not see him before we left the next day. When I got up that morning, I found a note from my dad. He asked if I would stick around long enough for the three of us to have lunch. I called him and readily agreed. I was pleasantly surprised at this unusual act coming from my father.

Marianna and I met my dad at the local restaurant in town, and we had a nice lunch. Dad informed me that he had decided to take the rest of the day off. I was surprised because, again, this was an unusual act coming from him. My hopes lifted just a bit. I was anticipating him asking us to stay just a little bit longer so that he could spend more time with us. Alas, he proceeded to talk about all the things he had to do that afternoon: get a tractor from the next town over; stop by the neighbor's to fix the manure spreader, etc. The old familiar feeling of him putting work before us came back again, and my heart sank. He must have seen the hint of disappointment on my face, because he quickly added, "I could put all that on hold if you wanted to come back to the farm for a little while." I readily agreed and could not wait to pay the bill and head back to the farm with him.

When we pulled into the driveway and got out of the vehicle, Marianna ran into the grass and started doing somersault after somersault. She had just perfected those in her gymnastics class and was proud to show off her skills. After about the third one, she yelled, "Papa, come do a sussersault with me!" To my surprise, my dad got in the grass on his hands and knees and did an awkward albeit sturdy somersault. Marianna laughed and laughed, yelling, "Again, Papa, again!" I watched them do somersaults and lie down in the grass together, laughing with each other. I was delighted to witness such a beautiful scene when God whispered to me, "This is how I created your father to be for *you*." Tears sprung to my eyes, and I felt my heart opening up like a flower. All the pent-up sadness, disappointment, and longing floated up into the air onto those words God had spoken to me. Happiness, love, fulfillment, and, of course, forgiveness replaced those feelings. God created my dad to be a father who would spend time with his children, one who would love and adore them in the time he would spend with them. The world molded my father so that he could not be those things for my brother and me back then. But he recognized his mistakes and is trying to be those things for my daughter.

And that is enough for now; that is more than enough.

Chapter

16

Missing the I Am,
Far Removed From Quiet,
a Jam-Packed Society, and
the Reverence for the Moment

Missing Buzz Lightyear

One day I was dropping Marianna off with my mom. Marianna handed her Buzz Lightyear doll to me. She told me to take it with me on my drive home so that I would not get lonely. I asked Marianna whether she was going to miss it.

She answered, "I won't be missing Buzz, Mom; I will be missing *you*."

L ORD, I MISS You."

"I am right here, My child," the Lord answers me.

"I know…but I still miss You."

"I have not gone anywhere. Your awareness of Me has dimmed," He points out.

A few seconds pass by as I mull this over in my soul.

He goes on, "I AM always moving about you. I AM moving with you, around you and through you. I AM still dancing. It is you who has forgotten the steps."

It is bedtime, and I am lying next to my daughter in her bed as Robert sits in the La-Z-Boy chair, reading her a fairy tale. I focus my attention on my soul and my two loved ones. I begin to feel the dance. I can feel God dancing among us. Marianna is drifting off to sleep; she lets out a little giggle. God has just danced with her. I crave this dance. I long for it. I am in *need* of it. Tears gather at the corners of my eyes. *How long have I gone without dancing with the Trinity?* I am pondering this in my mind when God inquires, "When have you had quiet time with Me?"

This question stops me. *When have I had quiet time with God?* I am not busy per se, but I am rarely alone either. My days are spent at home with Marianna, a rambunctious, only child who needs me as a playmate. When Robert is home, the three of us spend our time together. We believe strongly in family and put every ounce of our energy into it. We pray together, talk about God together, and do different ministries for God; it isn't like God isn't present in our lives. As I ponder, I realize that His presence has become dulled by the daily routine of life.

I have an antique pendulum clock that was given to me eons ago. It is wound with a key, and it ticks every time the pendulum swings to one side. It chimes on the hour, every hour. It has been with me since I was in college. I have had the clock so long that I no longer hear it. I do not hear the ticks. Sometimes I do not even hear it chime on the hour. Newcomers to our house will sometimes ask me to stop the clock because the ticking is so loud to them that they cannot focus on anything else. I look at them in surprise for I have forgotten that the clock was even moving.

I wonder if I am that way with God.

When I do notice the clock, I am in awe of its beauty. I love my clock. It belonged to a neighbor of mine whom I used to help care for in her elderly years. I remember noticing it every time I was in the kitchen because I used to think it was so loud. I always mentioned it when I was there. Maybe that was why she gave me the clock. She thought that I talked about it out of love rather than annoyance. When she died, the clock was passed down to me as a reminder of all the times we spent together. My feelings for the clock changed from annoyance to love because I now cherish that clock for what it represents and for how it has been with me through most of my adult life. When I stop to look and pay attention to the clock, I wonder how I can be so neglectful.

I believe my relationship with God has become similar to the way I treat my beautiful clock. He has been so ingrained in my life that sometimes I scarcely notice Him. He is right; my awareness of Him has dimmed just as my awareness of the clock has.

Yet I am not yet ready to admit defeat.

"Lord, I spend quiet time with You at church."

"Really! Yes, you do come early, but you talk to Robert and those around you. Then the music begins, and then Pastor Matt talks. When he is finished, you say a closing prayer, and then you leave to pick up Marianna. When do you have quiet time with Me?" the Lord responds respectfully to me.

Again I am stumped. And again I am asking myself, *When do I have quiet time with God?*

Tonight Robert has agreed to take Marianna to karate class so that I may have some quiet time to be alone with God. Five minutes after he leaves, he calls to let me know about some things that he has taken care of today. Fifteen minutes later I find myself upstairs, spending time with God. In the midst of prayer, He is telling me that I need to write. I know it is true, for I have put it off for far too long, and my heart has many things that need to be spoken. I ask God to join me (as always) in my writing time and head downstairs to the computer. As I type, I get two phone calls, and someone sends me Facebook chats, asking questions about an upcoming event. Even alone in the house I am not quiet and fully alone with God. My awareness of Him begins to dim again as I focus on these other things.

And I am annoyed.

How did we get to this noisy place?

How did we get so far removed from quiet? As I sit in my dining room, I can hear the furnace running, cars driving past, a snow blower running in the distance (for it is just after our ten-inch snow storm), the phone ringing once again but on my husband's phone (for he is now home), and my phone alerting me that I have received a new text message.

Research shows that little children breathe with their diaphragms. They know how to breathe deeply and fully. By the time *American* children reach the age of five, they are no longer diaphragm breathers; they are chest breathers. They breathe shallowly and only breathe as deep as their chest, almost like panting. The children tested in other countries remained diaphragm breathers well into their teens.

Why is that?

When I was a toddler, I was at home. I never went to day care or to preschool. I never took a dance class or signed up for soccer. I hung out at home, playing with my toys and being with my family. The only times we rushed to go somewhere were when we were running late to church. (Four people and one bathroom will do that from time to time.) Now as a mom of a toddler, I see that for some parents, rushing has become an art form. I signed Marianna up for dance/gymnastics class when she was two years old. In the summertime Marianna and I would leave half an hour before class and slowly walk the six or seven blocks to the class. We were usually the first ones there, and I would sit and watch the other moms come running in with their children, barely making it on time, and apologize for being late due to some other activity from which they had to pick up their children.

We have become a society of doing. Even Christian churches advocate it. The last time Robert and I were in church, there were at least ten minutes worth of announcements for different church activities in which people could get involved. When I talk with people from church, I am often asked about the Bible study to which I belong and the ministries in which I am participating to help serve the church and our community. When I answer that I am not involved in any activities beyond coming to church, I get looks of sadness and pity that I am somehow missing out on the great secret of life.

On Facebook I constantly see friends putting all the things they are doing or need to get done as their statuses. They somehow brag about being too busy to relax with a television show, to read a novel, or even to sleep well. And I wonder, *Is this how God intended for us to be?*

Now, don't get me wrong. I believe that we need to serve our communities and become involved. I also believe that we need to do it intentionally and not squander our time by having it filled with "things" to do. I do feel that is where we have gotten in our society, Christian or secular. We are a society that feels the need to have our calendars so jam-packed full of events, parties, places, and things to do, because if they are not, it somehow proves that we are lacking in some way. I, myself, do not buy that kind of merchandise. That does not mean that I have not fallen for their commercials once in a while; that is why there are times when I miss God even though He was never gone in the first place.

Yesterday Robert and I took Marianna up to the farm where my parents live. We took the Friday off and had the farm to ourselves since both my parents still work. Being near the Chicago area, they had quite a bit of snow. The three of us bundled up and headed for an outdoor winter adventure. We started at the playground area, swinging and looking at the snow cascading over the hillsides of farmland. We then walked under the evergreen trees, pretending that we were lost princesses and a prince, trying to find our way back to the castle as we fought off wildebeests (my parents' Saint Bernard). We walked the "crik" line and watched the water pass under the ice and float to its destination. We laughed, wrestled in the snow, loved on each other, and just spent time connecting with each other, nature, and God. Several moments of silence were spent at the "crik" because we felt the presence of God in that place. Even Marianna, who likes to talk, felt reverence for the moment heavily enough that she fell into silence.

I sat in the snow, looking at the water. "This is what You mean, Lord, isn't it?"

"Yes, My child."

"This *is* serving You, isn't it, Lord?"

"Yes, My child."

"This is how You originally meant for it to be, isn't it?"

"Ah, yes... and because it usually is not the way I intended it, that is why *I* most often miss *you*."

Chapter

17

❧

A Path of Blessing,
No More Peacemaker,
Sharpened Edges at Christmas, and
Celebration

———

Stuff vs. People

On the way home from the store, Marianna began to take off her shoes. I began to complain that we were only a few blocks from home and asked, "Can you please leave your shoes on, Marianna?"

I continued to complain when Marianna interrupted me and kindly said, "Mom, the world is not about shoes. It is not about stuff, but it *is* about people and their hearts."

I let her take her shoes off.

❧

O VER TEA ONE snow-laden afternoon, my beloved friend Sandi and I were discussing new topic ideas for the women's retreats that we lead. We wanted something that would be new for our returning guests as well as something that would not be too advanced for new people to join us. Sandi, being the sage that she is, began talking of an exercise she did years ago with her students called "Path of Blessings." She explained how we all have a path, a road that we are traveling on, and that path is made up of a series of decisions, whether those decisions were our own or pressed upon us by others. The exercise was to challenge ourselves to look at our paths and see how God has taken those decisions and moved us to where we needed to be. It was to see how God has taken tragedy and turned it into usefulness or joy down the road. It was seeing God's fingerprints on our lives and rejoicing in what He has done with them.

Sandi and I believed that we needed to practice what we preached, and that if we were to teach the "Path of Blessings" to others, we needed to have a good understanding of it in our own lives. I drove home slowly on the snowy highway with the idea beginning to grow in my mind. This was an exercise that I could sink my teeth into. I was excited to see how God would reveal His hand in my life. Now, I have always known God has had a hand on my life and has always been close beside me at all times. My relationship with God began at a little Lutheran church out in the middle of the country. It was the typical old country church with huge wooden doors, stained-glass windows, old wooden pews, and a wooden pulpit in the front for the preacher to bring his sermons home. Being of the Lutheran denomination, it was filled with ritual and reverence. I was about eight years old when the Holy Spirit first danced with me. I remember standing in one of the pews as we sang an old, slow hymn, which was played on an ancient pipe organ. I had my eyes closed and began to sway to the rhythm of the music. I thought to myself, "I want this." I did not fully understand what "this" was, but I knew that I wanted it. I asked, and I received.

At that time in my life I had closed myself in. I had learned early on that I was inconsequential in this world. I was living on the peripheral of life, trying hard not to take center stage; center stage is where the battlegrounds were. As I have mentioned before, my mother did not come from the greatest of backgrounds. She had a father who was an over-the-road truck driver and a mother who was never meant to be a mother at all. My mother had difficulty coping with having a family of her own, which led to depression and anxiety. My dad worked days and most nights and was not around to see what was happening. He too came from a rough upbringing, which led him to believe that a solid bank account would provide him comfort and safety in this world. That mentality came at a price. That price was the cost of his children.

I do not remember much before the age of eight, but I do remember that things were not right at home. My mom was a stay-at-home mom, but I do not ever really remember her being around. We lived in a farmhouse of average size but small enough that everyone knew where everyone else was. I remember my mom being there peripherally but not *with* me. I do not ever remember a time in which she snuggled with me on the couch, read to me, or just played on the floor. Tom and I would play together when we were younger, but as we got older, we grew our separate ways. I think it was because of how each of us had been treated back then. My mom and Tom would start fighting, over what I cannot remember. The fight would usually escalate to the point in which Tom would try to get away from her. I remember sitting in some corner as they fought. Tom would try to get away from her by going into different rooms, and Mom would follow, trying to get her point across. Tom's anger would build, and before it got too far, he would usually leave the house. I would sneak up to my room in hopes of going unnoticed.

My dad usually came home and into the house around dinnertime. He would come in to an earful about how horrible Tom was and how Mom could not handle him, so my dad would have to do something. The rest of the evening would be yelling while I, again, sat in a corner, praying not to be noticed. It did not happen every night, but it certainly happened enough to shape the inner workings of Tom and me. Tom became the quiet, disengaged, angry boy who kept everything inside until he exploded. I became the quiet, inward-turned, imaginative girl, conjuring up what my life would look like far away from there.

In later years Tom and I never got along. Tom always thought I got treated better because I was never in the center of the fights. But being ignored and not seen as important takes its own toll. When Tom became an adult, my mom began to feel guilty for how she had treated him and therefore began to have her life revolve around him. Common statements from my mom in regard to holidays were, "Well, you'll need to travel home because Tom likes to be home for Thanksgiving," or "Well, we're going to ask Tom what he wants to do since he works so hard." We always bended to what Tom wanted so as to appease my mother's guilt. I was single back then, so I would travel. I became the peacemaker. I became the one who made sure the family floated on smooth water. Those statements would always just solidify my unimportance within the family. My only place in it was the role of peacemaker, which I performed to a T. I hated and resented it.

When Robert came around, it was such a blessing. He saw

how my family was and began to show me what a healthy family actually consisted of. The first time we had a confrontation with my parents was during Thanksgiving when Marianna was four months old. It had been building with us for a while, beginning with Marianna's birth. When she was born, we were told that she had two holes in her heart. We were told moments before we were to take her home, and we were devastated. We were brand-new parents who had no idea what we were doing let alone how to take care of a baby whose heart was not fully developed. On the way home, Robert was brave enough to call both sets of parents to tell them the news. I was too emotional. His parents told us that they would support us no matter what; emotionally or financially, they would be there. My mom took the news and then told Robert she could not handle it right now and hung up. A week later I received a call from my dad, stating how upset my mom had been because I had not gotten in touch with her. He instructed me to call her to smooth things over. Ever the peacemaker I was.

So when Thanksgiving rolled around, my brother and his wife, Tammy, were having issues with my parents. They would not be attending dinner. Robert and I agreed to go with them to my parents' to talk about the issues and to instill some changes. My dad was receptive by the end and was willing to change. Mom stared at the floor, crying. However, changes were made, and things got better. Robert and I had a good relationship with them; healing in many realms was beginning to occur.

It is Christmas four years later, and my heart bleeds. Old patterns have reemerged, and once again I feel forced to the back burner while plans are changed to fit what Tom wants. Now, I have no anger toward Tom over this. Most of the time he has no idea that my parents give me excuses. It is my parents dealing with their demons through pleasing Tom. God no longer wants me to be silent. My role of peacemaker in this family has come to its end. I lay out for my parents what is hurting my heart and what they need to do to heal it. They are defensive from the start. My pleas and requests are met with negotiation tactics. The response is e-mail laden with either guilt or outrage. I am numb to both.

I would have thought that this heartbreak would dull the beauty of Christmas. However, it has sharpened its edges. The lights on the tree are brighter and more succinct. The Christmas music playing in my kitchen is deeper and richer than I have ever heard it before. My understanding of Christmas is being etched deeper into my soul, and I am filled. Jesus came because of suffering. Jesus came to rectify all that had been done. That beautiful baby who was born reminds us that not all has been lost. His birth is a promise fulfilled, and so I am grateful that this time of hurt has happened over Christmas. Christmas is not for the happy, sentimental, abundant times for which we so often mistake Christmas to represent. Christmas is for the broken, down-trodden, lost, and hopeless ones.

It also reminds me that this is not about me. It is about God's story of healing and redemption. God has pointed me in the direction of being a therapist, teacher, and mentor for a moment like this. This is the path He set out for me. He has had me work in prisons with offenders to become strong and open to negotiation, guilt, and defensiveness—the stuff I am coming up against today with my parents. God knew this time would come when I would be at odds with my parents and need the strength and knowledge that I have in order to bring about healing. The healing I am talking about is healing my parents' relationship with God. They have long forgotten Him, and God is calling them home. He wants them back. So, my story is not my story at all but God's. This is His story of redemption and healing. My story, like all stories, is much bigger than I am. The story of the Israelites was not really about them but about God working through them. The story of Noah and the flood is not really about Noah but about God restoring mankind and making His covenant with us through Noah. My part in this story is choosing to allow God to work through me, for we all have free will and can choose our own path.

My brother has chosen not to walk this path with me. He chooses to stay on the sidelines and watch where this path might lead us. I choose to be an agent of God. I choose to let Him lead me wherever the path may go. I choose it not for myself but for my daughter. Unknowingly, my mom passed on the generational sin that she received from her mother. I refuse to do that. Exodus 34:6–7 says, "The Lord, the Lord, the compassionate and gracious God, slow to anger, abounding in love and faithfulness, maintaining love to thousands, and forgiving wickedness, rebellion and sin. Yet he does not leave the guilty unpunished; he punishes the children and their children for the sin of the fathers to the third and fourth generation." He says it again in Numbers 14:18 and again in Exodus 20:5. God wants to make it clear to us that if we don't cut off the generational sins, they will continue to our children and to their children. I refuse to give mine to my daughter. And so I charge forth on my path of blessing. I have no idea where it will lead me, but I do know that God will take me to a place I never could have dreamed. His imagination is far better than mine.

As for my parents, they have come to counseling with me, listened to my heart, and have begun the necessary changes in order for us to heal. I could not be prouder of them. They have been willing to hear my heart and do what it will take to rectify it. They have a strong desire not to carry forward the negative traditions of their forefathers. Their hearts are open, and I am at peace.

Sadly, my brother remains a quiet entity in this process, yet that is OK, for we all choose our own path.

As for me, I choose the path of blessing, which is Christ's path.

And I celebrate.

Chapter

18

SpongeBob,
Allowing It to Be Given,
Burning Bushes,
Loving Whispers, and
Opening Hearts

Right Next To

Marianna said to me, "Mom, you are forever in my heart. Right next to Jesus. That's the best place to be I think!"

THE OTHER DAY I was sitting on the floor with my two-and-a-half-year-old daughter, Marianna, while she was watching *SpongeBob SquarePants*. Now, when SpongeBob is on, no one is allowed to talk. If you so much as look like you might say a phrase or two, she will scold you and let you know that there will be consequences if you do. SpongeBob is her buddy, and nobody better mess with her time with SpongeBob and the gang! Sitting there with her standing next to me and her arms wrapped around my neck, I could not help but whisper in her ear over and over again, "I love you. I love you. I love you."

Over and over I whispered closely into her ear, "I love you. I love you. I love you." I was not sure how long I could keep it up because I was sure it would interrupt her ability to concentrate on her show; however, I kept going. I repeated it again and again and again. Now, one thing I should mention about my daughter is that she is someone who definitely knows what she wants and is not afraid to let you know it. She is two and a half and has a very good sense of who she is. And as I stated before, SpongeBob is one of her favorites. So I had quit whispering the "I love yous" in her ear for fear of reprimand. Instead, she pulled on my neck, forced my head near her ear, and whispered, "Again, Mom. Again." She never once took her eyes off the television screen. So for the rest of that episode along with another show, Mari and I held each other in front of the television while I continuously whispered "I love you" into her ear. She never once took her eyes or concentration off of the television, but she knew I was there. She craved for me to continue my utterances.

On a deeper level, she knew her soul needed it, wanted it.

And she allowed it to be given.

She even asked for it.

Now Marianna, if I haven't said it before, is very strong-willed. She is also one who is too busy and who enjoys life too much to sleep. So one evening when it was time to go to bed, Marianna decided that she was going to stay up. We sat on the rocker together and read some books in hopes of calming her down and tiring her out. When the book reading was over, the tantrums began. I held her across her middle while she screamed, kicked, and hit me. I knew that eventually she would wear herself out, and I continued to hold her while she physically and emotionally let loose on me. After about fifteen minutes (which felt like an hour), she finally collapsed into my lap and started crying. In between sobs, she would say that she was sorry and didn't mean to hurt me.

To me, it was over and done with. All was forgiven. I held her to me and whispered over and over to her, "I love you. I love you. I love you." I continued to say it to her until I felt her body go limp and heard a faint snore in my ear.

As for me, I am not always a wonderful mom who knows just what to do in every circumstance. I certainly have my faults and express them from time to time. One of these times was yesterday afternoon.

The last few nights Marianna had not been sleeping all that well. She would wake every couple of hours, screaming and crying. (She is a very vivid dreamer.) It would take a good hour to put her back down, only to have it happen again. My husband and I took turns dealing with her, but I had difficulty going back to sleep after an episode (probably because I knew it would happen again). So by yesterday morning I was exhausted! You know that type of exhausted when you put your pants on before your underwear? Well, that was me. I knew that if Marianna and I were going to function well the rest of the day, we would need a nap.

As I said before, Mari hates to sleep; when naptime came, so did the tantrums. Only I was not as patient this time. I threw a tantrum of my own; I yelled, spanked her bottom, and walked away when I knew she needed me. Not one of my proudest moments, and certainly one that haunted me the rest of the day.

Later on I was lying down on the couch with tears streaming down my face because of how I acted toward the gift that God had bestowed upon me. I felt like a horrible mother who was not deserving of something so precious. Earlier I had apologized to Marianna and made up with her. She easily forgave, as all kids do, and went on to some toy she found in her playroom. She and I were the only ones home, but I knew that God had witnessed my actions and knew that He could not be too happy with them or me. As the tears flowed, I poured my regrets out to Him, apologized for my behavior, and wondered how He could ever forgive me.

After I cried and poured out my heart, I just lay there in silence. And soon I heard a faint echo:

"I love you. I love you. I love you."

I knew in that moment that it was over and done with. All was forgiven. Oh, how those words filled my heart and overflowed through the rest of my body! I was restored. I was renewed and lifted up. I got up off the couch and played dollies with my daughter.

How often do we crave for our Father to whisper those words into our ears? How often do we cry out to Him to hear those words without even knowing it? How often are we too distracted by the world or our own mess to even notice that that is exactly what He is doing?

After the SpongeBob afternoon show with my daughter, I started paying soulful attention to those moments in which my mind was distracted. I was making scones, and I heard, "I love you, My child." I heard it again as I was putting a load of laundry in, when I was getting the mail, and when I was looking up music on iTunes. Once I paid attention, I heard those words everywhere. And I realized how much I needed them.

Rob Bell talks about burning bushes and how they might be all around us, yet we are so distracted that we would just walk right on by them.[1] I think of that in this situation. *How many times has God whispered "I love you" in my ear, only to have it be blown away by others' words or by my mind's distractions?* I believe that there are burning bushes all around us, and I am learning through my daughter how prevalent and amazing they are. I am learning through her to open my eyes and notice them. I am sure that I am still walking past many other burning bushes, but I am excited and renewed to even come upon this one! It makes me yearn for God even more. He loves and yearns for me. How incredible is that!

It is an amazing thing to hear your child tell you that she loves you; it is a different type of amazing to hear it from your spouse or someone you love. It is beyond amazing to hear it from the Creator of the universe. This life-giving force loves you! The Creator who made the plants, water, sky, and heavens specifically and mindfully loves you!

And He is constantly telling us that; may our hearts be open just enough to hear it.

Epilogue

AFTER DOING SOME preschool work with Marianna, I let her play for a while in the living room while I folded laundry. I could hear Marianna talking up a storm, telling someone all about her day, and asking if the person would like to join her for a tea party. I figured she was talking to one of her many stuffed animals that she usually has attending her tea parties. As I walked past the living room, I looked in and saw Marianna sitting at her table alone. There were no stuffed animals, only one empty chair sitting across from her. This seemed a bit strange for my daughter, so I stopped and quietly watched what she was doing.

"Would You like some tea, Jesus?" Marianna asked. Jesus must have wanted some, for she poured a cup and set it by the empty chair. "Jesus, I made these cookies myself. Aren't You proud of me?" Jesus must have been, for her face beamed with happiness as she set down pretend cookies in front of Him. She sat and pretended to eat and drink as she held a conversation with Jesus. A little while later, Marianna excused herself from her table and came over by me. "Mom, can you please bring the iPod in here?" she asked. I replied, "Of course, but why?" Marianna said, "Well, Jesus just asked if I would like to dance, and I would, but we don't have any music." As I put on some music, I was able to sit back and watch my child. She bowed before Jesus and then took His hands and began dancing around our living room floor. She twirled and spun, as all little girls love to do. She curtsied between each dance and again began to twirl around the dance floor of our living room.

She and Jesus danced to the likes of Sting, Van Morrison, Jason Mraz, and Norah Jones. After a while Marianna approached me, "Mom, Jesus asked if you would like to join us." I bowed before my daughter and joined them on the dance floor. I closed my eyes as I held on to my daughter's hand. I floated, swayed, and glided over the dance floor as I felt Jesus and the Holy Spirit dance around me. It was one of the most peaceful and loving moments I had ever felt.

When putting Marianna to bed that night, I asked her what her favorite part of the day was. She answered without hesitation, "When Jesus came down from heaven and had a playdate with me." I asked her if Jesus came down a lot to have playdates with her. She answered, "Jesus comes to play with me a lot, but He also takes me up to heaven to play too. We have the best time! Jesus is a funny guy! He tells me lots of things. He told me that He is sad because most people when they grow up forget to have playdates and dance with Jesus. He wants you to dance with Him more, Mom." Without any more discussion, Marianna gave me a kiss and rolled over to go to sleep.

I have to admit, I was a bit taken aback by this. I always thought that I had a good relationship with my Maker. I spend time with the Bible; I pray and talk to God about various issues. This was going to be another issue that I would discuss with Him as well. As I rocked with Marianna, I brought the subject up with God. I asked Him to reveal to me what He was trying to tell me. After a few moments of silence, I received this memory:

I was about eight years old, standing in the middle of a wheat field. It was summer, and the sun was warm on my shoulders. A gentle breeze tickled my face, and the wheat was swaying with the gentle wind as it played around my legs. I could hear birds singing as I watched them have fun in the air. I remember beginning to sway with the wheat, closing my eyes, feeling all that was around me.

In the present, God whispered, "That is Me. All of it: the wheat, the sun, the breeze, the birds. You were dancing with *Me* in that field." A smile spread across my face as understanding filled my heart. "Come dance with Me again, My child. Close your eyes, feel the rhythm and dance. I am in the rhythm, in the movement. Always. Just look around, and I will show you."

———

After seeing a client today, I had an hour break before I had to see my next client. I walked from the front office, to the back of our house, to the kitchen. When I got into the kitchen, I heard music playing and saw Robert holding our daughter as he danced with her. When he looked up and saw me come in the room, he quietly extended his hand. I joined in the dance of our own trio. I closed my eyes and felt every movement. I was aware of those around me whom I loved most in this world: my family, my God, my Jesus, and the Holy Spirit within me, swaying in rhythm with me. I finally understood, and all was right with the world.

Notes

Author's Note

1. Sybil MacBeth, Praying in Color: Drawing a New Path to God (Brewster, MA: Paraclete Press, 2007), 44.

2. Timothy Keller, The Reason for God: Belief in an Age of Skepticism (New York, NY: Penguin Group Inc., 2008), 224.

Chapter 2
Did Jesus Want the Night Off? Refusing to Order Pizza, Forgetting Our Equation, and the Sum is Greater than Our Parts

1. Rob Bell, Sex God: Exploring the Endless Connections between Sexuality and Spirituality (Grand Rapids, MI: Zondervan Publishing, 2007), 63.

Chapter 3
Blaming Our Families, Happiness Skyrockets, Watering Camels for Love, and a Door in a Remote, Sleepy Town

1. Sark, Fabulous Friendship Festival: Loving Wildly, Learning Deeply, Living Fully with Our Friends (New York: Crown Publishing Group, 2007).

Chapter 7
Knowing the Outcome Before You Begin, the Destination Beyond, Expert-Level Mudslides, and Showing Me the Way

1. Rob Bell, Velvet Elvis (Grand Rapids, MI: Zondervan Publishing, 2005), 158.

2. David Guralnik, Webster's New World Dictionary (New York, NY: Simon & Schuster Publishing, 1982), 7.

3. Ibid.

4. Retrieved from www.wikipedia.org/etymology/guide

Chapter 13
Sighing the Little-Kid Sigh, No Need to Pray Any Longer, Unworthiness Baked Right in, and Amazing Tutelage

1. Calvin Miller, *The Path of Celtic Prayer: An Ancient Way to Everyday Joy* (Downers Grove, IL: InterVarsity Press, 2007).

Chapter 18
SpongeBob, Allowing It to Be Given, Burning Bushes, Loving Whispers, and Opening Hearts

1. *Breathe*, Perf. Rob Bell. Nooma, 2006, DVD

About the Author

ONIQUE JESIOLOWSKI, MA, RYT, is a Christian therapist in her own private practice, Lamplighter Counseling Center. She holds a masters of counseling degree from Indiana Wesleyan University. Monique has been working in the counseling field for twenty years, specializing in helping everyday people find God's true design for who they are. Monique was a crisis center hotline director before becoming a crisis counselor and therapist, working extensively with couples, adults, adolescents, and children in residential, community, and correctional settings.

Monique is an experienced national speaker at a variety of conferences on the topics of living out one's Christian views, coping with abuse, understanding addictions, finding balance, and overcoming strongholds. She co-facilitates Christian women's retreats, playdates with God, in her community and abroad; they are designed to provide insight, joy, peace, fellowship, and creative outlets. She designed and teaches Christian Restorative Body Prayer in addition to being a certified yoga instructor.

Monique is an adjunct professor for Indiana Wesleyan University, where she teaches marriage and family counseling courses. Monique is happily married to the love of her life, a fellow therapist and colleague. At Lamplighter Counseling, Monique and her husband use a uniquely developed tandem-counseling strategy, which provides a husband-and-wife therapist team in every session with the couples to help each partner feel heard and understood while role-modeling healthy relationship practices.

Monique has an amazing five-year-old daughter, Marianna Thunder, who is filled with the Holy Spirit. Monique loves herb gardening, praying in color, reading books, and homeschooling her daughter. God designed Monique to be a mother, a wife, a teacher, a professor, a facilitator, a speaker, a counselor, and a therapist, but she is still learning how to be a dancer.

Contact the Author

*I would love to hear how God is dancing in your life.
I would also love to continue sharing
my current melodies and dance steps with you.*

*Visit me at: www.lamplightercounseling.com,
sign up on the website for my quarterly newsletter,
or email me at:
lamplightercounseling@yahoo.com.*

We are all part of the dance. Won't you join me?

Lamplighter Counseling was established in 2006 as a Christian Life Center.

The staff is comprised of Therapist Monique Jesiolowski, MA, RYT, and her husband, Robert, a Licensed Clinical Social Worker. Together they have more than thirty years of combined clinical experience. They specialize in using their specially developed Co-Therapy model with couples, where both Robert and Monique together counsel and guide couples through the therapeutic experience.

Other services include individual psychotherapy for children, adolescents, and adults, as well as group psychotherapy, pre-marital and marital therapy, family therapy, e-mail counseling and counseling workshops. Individualized Christ-centered Body Prayer classes are offered to fit client needs and schedules. Psycho-educational presentations are available as well.

If you would like further information please contact us at 765-499-1974, or by e-mail: lamplightercounseling@yahoo.com, or through our website: www.lamplightercounseling.com.